A Practical Guide to
Flexible Working Hours

Stephen J. Baum and W. McEwan Young

A Practical Guide to
Flexible
Working
Hours

Stephen J Baum
and
W McEwan Young

Kogan Page

19610

25814

First published 1973 by
Kogan Page Limited
116a Pentonville Road London N1 9JN

Setting by Gyro Repro, Maidstone, Kent

Printed in Great Britain by Lowe & Brydone (Printers) Ltd Thetford, Norfolk

SBN 85038 014 6

Authors' Preface

During the latter part of 1972, the authors were involved, to a varying degree, in the design of a flexible working hour system in a company in the East Midlands. Following a successful installation, in both the administrative and technical and production areas, it became clear that there was a tremendous interest in fwh schemes and we were inundated with requests for information from organisations considering the possibility of applying it in their own situation. By early 1973 it had become obvious to us that there was a need for some sort of definitive treatment of fwh. Most of the literature available was inadequate and organisations were finding it costly and time-wasting to generate information from scratch. This book is an attempt to meet the needs of such organisations.

Our intention has been to cover fwh at as many levels as possible, so that it can be read, with profit, by those whose interest has been aroused and who want to obtain a general appreciation; by those whose interest have taken them to the point where they wish to conduct a feasability study; and by those who, committed to an installation, need a detailed knowledge of the mechanics of the system and the problems which are likely to arise.

We hope we have succeeded in meeting these objectives.

Loughborough June 1973.   Stephen J. Baum.
                                                           W. McEwan Young.

ACKNOWLEDGEMENTS

The authors acknowledge gratefully the help and contributions received from
Addo Ltd; Allen & Hanburys Ltd; Association of Scientific, Technical & Management Staffs; Bakelite Xylonite Ltd; Blick Time Recorders Ltd; British Olivetti Ltd; Essex River Authority; Feedback Data Ltd; Hasler (Great Britain) Ltd; Hengstler Flextime Ltd; International Time Recording Co Ltd; Legal & General Assurance Society Ltd; London & Manchester Assurance Co Ltd; Northgate Instruments Ltd; Russell Greer & Associates Ltd; Simplex Time Recorder Co; Telephone Rentals Ltd and the organisations and Trade Unions (other than those mentioned above) who participated in the surveys.

In addition, we would like particularly to thank Messrs. T. Copson, M. Dewar, A. MacDonald, G. Miller, P. Paulsom, L. Reeve, M. Reynolds and the Executive Directors, management & staff of Riker Laboratories.

Finally, acknowledgement must be made of the help and encouragement given us by our wives; their forebearance, critical comment and practical assistance in draft typing of the copy, made it possible for us to produce this book much more smoothly than would otherwise have been possible.

S.J.B. & W.McY.

SPECIAL NOTE
The trade marks Flextime and Gleitzeit are the Registered Trade Marks of Hengstler G.B. Ltd, and the sole registered users thereof are Hengstler Flextime Ltd.

Contents

1. A New Approach

Work in a Historical Perspective

If we examine the concept of work in historical perspective, we find that man's thinking about it has tended to vary with changes in the structure of human society. To the ancient Greeks work was simply a curse, and this view appears to have been shared by the Romans and Hebrews of that time. The 'Protestant Ethic', ushered in by Luther and elaborated by Calvin, swept away the distinctions between worldly labour and service to God and this paved the way for a new man, hard-working, active and above all, austere, who firmly believed that redemption in the eyes of the Lord could only be sought through work. It would be uncharitable to suggest that these early religious reformers were motivated, in their theological thinking, by the needs of an industrial system which was emerging in human society. On the other hand, it cannot be denied that their intervention was opportune, for what the modern factory system required, in addition to new technologies and capital accumulation, was a disciplined, hard-working and obedient servant, in place of the highly independent artisan who had characterised the Guild system. Intermittent service had no place in the mills and mines of early industrial society; the work of all, master and servant, had to be methodical and regular. If costs were to be reduced and output maximised, all had to start when the hooter blew and all must labour until the signal was given to cease. Thus, into the management control system of industrial society was built the concept of a fixed working day, and if, through social reform, trade union action and enlightened employer attitudes, the length of that day has been progressively reduced, the idea of a fixed starting time and a fixed finishing time for those who labour has tended to remain inviolate.

Changing Attitudes to Work

Attitudes to work have altered significantly in the past fifty years, and the rate of change has accelerated in the past decade. The Victorians soon appreciated that the promise of a place in the

11

hereafter as a reward for good and faithful service was less moti-
vating than the acquisition of possessions in the present, (imperfect
as it might be) and, in a developing consumer society, man was
induced to replace a desire for salvation with a desire for material
goods. It would be trite to pretend that the motive of 'self-better-
ment', is no longer a dominant force in our society. In market-
orientated consumer societies it remains a main-spring of the
economy. But it can also be argued that modern man now seeks
more from work than the satisfaction of *extrinsic* values. If work
is to be a satisfying enriching experience then it must have *intrinsic*
values; and if there is one aspect of work that has received more
than its fair share of research in the past thirty years, it is that
aspect concerned with the reduction of alienation and the development of job satisfaction. Running like a thread through the
philosophy of early radicals like William Morris to the modern
theories of Maslow, McGregor and Hertzberg, is the theme that, if
man is to find self-actualization in work, then he must be in a
position to exercise *choice,* make *decisions* and assume *responsibility.* Companies now spend vast sums of money in an attempt to
provide the necessary structural conditions for the development of
a mature, satisfied and integrated work force who find such
intrinsic values within the work situation itself.

And as the rate of technological advance increases, the solution to
this problem is the more eagerly sought. The whole ethos of
industrial society is continually being challenged by the conflicting
demands for more material goods and services on the one hand and
the individual's need to express himself as a complete person in
control of his personal situation on the other. There is no need to
re-state the problem; it is one with which everyone, management
and workforces alike, is intimately involved.

The Fixed Working Day

Most of the work carried out in this field has concentrated on re-
shaping job content or task structure, at both the individual and
group level, and significant changes have been initiated in production methods and organisational design in an attempt to provide
a new framework for the individual in work situations in large
industrial and commercial organisations. The announcement by
Volvo that they are to abandon their assembly line for a new
concept in car production which will involve their workers in

12

group situations is an example of the extent to which the modern business enterprise is prepared to accommodate the socio/psychological requirements of their work force.

It is strange, therefore, that in an area where discretion and choice might have been introduced into the work situation at comparatively little cost, the situation with regard to the fixed working day has remained frozen for over 200 years. With few exceptions, the work forces of industrial and commercial organisations, in both the capitalist and mixed economies and communist blocs, have been denied discretion as to the times at which they can start work and the times at which they might finish. The factory hooter has been replaced by the more ubiquitous time clock and the 'knocker-up' by the modern alarm, but despite technological and ideological change, one characteristic of industrial society remains constant. The location of the working day is rigidly fixed in time.

Changing Structure of Modern Life

Now technological and social change in society has been considerable and if, so far, we have concentrated on the changing attitudes of the individual to intrinsic values in the work situation, this is not to belittle the extrinsic factors which have tended to make life more complex for modern industrial man. These would include —

Changing patterns of national population distribution
Cities have become larger and sprawl outwards into the countryside. In Britain, for example, the North East becomes depopulated while the South East expands round the conurbation of Greater London. The new electronic industries of the developing post-industrial society vie with the older established firms for a place near the Channel seaboard, and, despite attempts by successive governments to halt the tide, the population drifts inexorably to the southern half of Britain.

Changing concentrations of employment
Productivity, efficiency, rationalisation and cost effectiveness demand that large numbers of individuals be concentrated in one particular locale, and it is not unusual, in modern industrial society, for up to 10,000 individuals to be concentrated, for work purposes, in an area of under ten acres.

13

Changing patterns of employment
Under the impact of technological advance, work loads for individuals, in complex modern organisations, are rarely constant; they have a specific rhythm, either on a daily or longer term basis, and are characterised by peaks and troughs.

Changing patterns of work/home relationships
No longer do work forces live within spitting distance of the factory in which they work. The move from the centre of our cities is ever-outwards and all long to live in the semi-green of suburbia. Yet the factories themselves are slow to move. A Victorian edifice may not be ideal, but as building costs soar, the reasons for staying put become more convincing.

Changing patterns of transport
The motor car has largely taken over as a method of private transport for employees, management and work forces alike. Once the preserve of the few, it now threatens to choke our cities in the chaos of diurnal rush hour traffic. Nor is the public transport commuter in a happier position as he joins the lemming-rush on rail, tube or bus.

Changing patterns in labour markets
Work is no longer the preserve of the male in the family. Women, both married and single, now form a significant fraction of the total labour force in most organisations and, in some, form a majority.

Changing social attitudes
The Welfare State has to be fed. Appointments with dentists, doctors, psychologists, specialists, out-patient departments, family planners and marriage advisers have to be kept. Work people need more time to attend to their physical, social and psychological needs and the practitioners they wish to see no longer consult in the evenings. And few companies, save the giant corporations, can afford to lay on such a comprehensive service that all the welfare needs of their employees can be met on the premises.

The Developing Crisis

These changes have precipitated a crisis for society in general and

for industrial and commercial organisations in particular. It is a
crisis which is characterised, in the great conurbations of Western
industrial society, by a frustrated individual, travelling into the
city, along with tens of thousands of others, on an overcrowded
public transport system which cannot cope with the constraint of
the fixed starting time for the working day. If he is 'lucky' enough
to work for a company who have themselves moved out from the
city to a green-fields site, then he will probably arrive in a private
car in company with hundreds of others, and will find himself
fighting for access to the car park. If he has to make a visit to the
doctor or dentist he may, according to his position in the company,
have to ask for time off, for which he may or may not be paid.
If he has personal problems which necessitate a visit to a solicitor
or builder or hospital, he may have to lose a working day, and the
goodwill of his superiors, in order to do this. If he is late for work,
due to circumstances beyond his control (strikes on public transport, bad weather conditions, traffic congestion) he faces the
necessity of an apology or the ignominy of a reprimand.

If he is an individual who is a slow starter in the morning, he may
find that he never reaches his peak work-rate until later in the
day. Or, if his work load fluctuates, he may find himself, after a
frustrating morning journey in winter conditions, sitting idly at his
desk or bench, for the first two hours of the day. If the individual
is a married woman, the problems multiply — hairdresser, shopping,
children; how to fit it all in when the work day is fixed and the
lunch hour is inflexible? And at the end of the day, the problems
interchange. To stay on and complete the work load? (do they
extinguish the lights at 5 pm? do they pay overtime? can I have
time off in lieu?), or to plunge out into the maelstrom of com-
muters who simultaneously fight their way, by tube, bus and car,
from work place to home?

The situation demands a solution, both in terms of society, the
company and the individual. Society, because it cannot afford the
resources to cope with the surges of humanity which take place at
work start and *work finish* times. The company, because it does
not have the resources to cope with its employees' failure to
adjust to the transport problem, the individual metabolism
problem, the work load problem and the employees' personal
problems. The individual because he *is* an individual, not a cipher.
Denied any discretion in how he should organise his working day
to meet his physiological, sociological and psychological needs, he
finds himself in a constant state of tension and stress.

15

Staggered Hours

Defining the problem did not, in itself, throw up a ready solution. The alterations to the fixed working day seemed limited; after all, complete choice by the individual was not possible. Operational requirements necessitated some control by the company and this was accepted by employees and trade unions alike. Some alleviation of the stress created by peak hour travelling could be arrived at by a *staggered working day* system and experiments were introduced, particularly in conurbations, in which the conventional working day (say 08.00hrs to 17.00hrs) was offset, in relation to other companies, by advancing the day (07.00hrs to 16.00hrs) or retarding the day, (09.00hrs to 18.00hrs). It has to be acknowledged that this had a limited success, yet many of the problems remained unsolved. Customers found it difficult to adjust to a situation in which the company was out of step with everyone else. In commercial undertakings using an 'advanced' stagger, work load problems arose in connection with mail deliveries. And for the individual, the tyranny of timekeeping, the difficulties of 'time off', and above all, the absence of choice, remained as insoluble as ever.

A Major Breakthrough

Staggered working hours made a contribution in terms of the societal problem of travelling to and from work, but the major breakthrough in thinking was delayed until the mid 1960's and, when it came, like all revolutionary ideas, it was amazingly simple in concept. The idea of flexible working hours is credited to a management consultant in Konigswinter, a small town on the Rhine, near Bonn. Mrs Christel Kammerer hit on the idea that the fixed working day, with its rigid start and finish times, could be replaced by a working day in which the hours of work should be *flexible* instead of *fixed*.

The fact that the flexibility is generally built in to flexible bands at the beginning and end of the day and that a core time (when it is mandatory for all employees to be present), is interposed between the flexible bands, makes the system attractive to the company which requires its work force to be present for the main part of the working day. On the other hand, by allowing the work force to start or finish when they wish (subject to certain constraints), individual frustrations in terms of travelling, work loads, personal needs and so on, can be resolved and, by further refining the system in terms of debit and credit hours against a standard, a new concept of working time and free time can be introduced.

The Idea Spreads

Since its introduction by Messerschmitt Bolkow in 1968 in Otto-brun, the scheme's adoption in Germany has accelerated to a point where the number of German companies involved now exceeds 3,500. These include organisations in —

Banking (Commerzbank, Dusseldorf with 1800 employees)

Manufacture (Boehringer Mannheim of Mannheim with 3,000 employees) (Brown Boveri of Switzerland with 16,000 employees)

Service (Deutsche Fina with 230 employees)

Retail Distribution (Haidt, Fashion Store in Tubingen).

The Germans call it *Gleitzeit* (gliding time) and from Germany the idea has spread quickly through Europe, with installations already made in France, Austria, Swedish and Swiss companies. It is perhaps surprising that the USA has tended to trail behind in this particular innovation. Nevertheless, by 1970, at least one company, the Hecon Corporation in Eatontown NJ implemented the system on a trial basis. It appears that the idea was a complete success and in October of that year the firm decided to implement the scheme in all its departments/divisions. Thus, it may not be long before the innovation extends on the American continent and this is sub-stantiated by reports, received by the authors in March 1973, of trial schemes which are being conducted by four companies on the East Coast of USA.

There are also reports of awakening interest in the Far East and Australian continent. According to Riley [1], the Japanese are so keenly interested that they have sent a television crew to London to record some of the experiments taking place in the UK. And from Australia comes a report that their first experiment will start shortly with a limited pilot scheme (covering 150 employees) in the Australian Department of Supply, Melbourne.

What is abundantly clear is that *Gleitzeit, Horaire Dynamique, Orario Flessibile, Flexsibel Werktijd, Jisashukin,* or just plain Flexible Working Hours, is a concept which is quite unique in the history of employer-employee relationships. What is perhaps more difficult to understand is why such a simple concept, with so

17

universal appeal has not been thought of before now.

Development in the UK

Until the latter part of 1972, application of flexible working hours in the UK was extremely limited. It is difficult to be precise on a matter which is not covered by statistical returns, but allowing for the level of generalisation acceptable in management journals and newspapers one can identify a pattern of growing interest and experimentation among British companies. For example, at the beginning of 1972, Duff Hart Davis[2] in a report, mentioned only five companies experimenting with flexible working hours despite the fact that, at that time, a leading manufacturer of time recording equipment used with the scheme reported over 1,000 enquiries. In June 1972, Bishop[3], spoke of 7 companies with a combined payroll of 1,300 employees, who were experimenting with the scheme on a trial basis, and alleged that the largest single experiment covered only 300 employees. Two months later Deeson [4], identified 9 companies and by January of 1973 Bolton [5], was talking of 12 companies experimenting with flexible working hours. Whatever the absolute figures may be, there is strong evidence that the latest figures (at the time of writing, May 1973, at least 200 organisations with nearly 50,000 employees are involved) indicate an accelerating interest in flexible hours and it is clear that an increasing number of companies, under a variety of pressures, are prepared to experiment with a view to eliminating that sacred cow of industrial society, the fixed working day.

(1)   Riley N. *Daily Telegraph* 4th April 1973.
(2)   Duff Hart-Davis *Sunday Telegraph* 27 February 1972
(3)   Bishop, T. *Personnel Management* June 1972 p.36
(4)   Deeson, A.F.L. *Works Management* July/August 1972 p.3
(5)   Bolton J.H. *Management Today* January 1973 p.29.

2. Basic Principles of Flexible Working Hours

The essential aim of the flexible working day is to replace the traditional fixed times at which an employee starts and finishes work by allowing him a limited choice in deciding his starting and finishing times of work each day. The choice of starting and finishing times can be as flexible as the company wishes them to be. The simplest version allows an employee to start and finish at times decided by him, and within limits set by his employer, providing that he works the contracted number of hours per day. This is the basic concept that will be developed in this book.

In developing the concept we shall be using terms that take on special meanings. These terms will now be defined.

Flexible Working Day — Basic Definitions

Fixed Working Day   A day with fixed starting and finishing times between which an employee undertakes to work a contracted number of hours.

Daily Contracted Hours   The number of daily hours of attendance at work to fulfil the individual contract of employment (or relevant collective agreement).

Flexible Working Day   A day without fixed starting and finishing times, but containing flexible time periods and core time periods.

Flexible Time   The periods at the beginning and end of each day during which the individual is free to choose when he or she arrives and leaves.

Bandwidth   The bandwidth is the time between the earliest permitted start of work and the latest permitted finish.

Core Time   The middle part of the day, excluding the lunch break, when *all* employees must be at their job. Thus attendance in core time is mandatory.

The Fixed Working Day and the Flexible Working Day

The differences between the fixed and basic flexible working day (with a fixed lunch break) are illustrated in the following two examples.

Fig.2.1

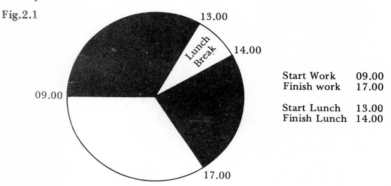

Start Work	09.00
Finish work	17.00
Start Lunch	13.00
Finish Lunch	14.00

A company's normal working day is from 09.00 hrs to 17.00 hrs with a fixed lunch break of one hour. This means that the contracted daily attendance hours are seven. *(See Fig.2.1.)* The employee has no choice as to when he starts or finishes work. Any deviation from these times must normally be pre-sanctioned by management. Failure to record 7 hours daily can lead to sanctions (loss of pay, reprimand, curtailment of privileges, etc) and these are normally exercised at the discretion of management.

The company introduces a flexible working day and allows its employees a flexible time band of one-and-a-half hours at the beginning and end of each working day. Employees may start work between 08.00 hrs and 09.30 hrs and finish at any time between 16.30 hrs and 18.00 hrs.

The core time is from 09.30 hrs to 16.30 hrs minus the lunch break and, under normal circumstances, all employees must be present during this time. *(See Fig.2.2.)* Out of this core time of seven hours, they are required to take a fixed lunch break of one hour.

Effective core time is thus six hours and if the employee wishes to work his contracted daily attendance hours of seven, he must work a total of at least one hour in flexible time.

Fig.2.2

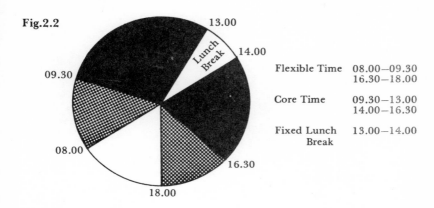

Flexible Time	08.00—09.30
	16.30—18.00
Core Time	09.30—13.00
	14.00—16.30
Fixed Lunch Break	13.00—14.00

Example 1   An employee arrives and is ready to start work at 08.30 hrs, half-an-hour earlier than his previous starting time of 09.00 hrs. He takes the fixed hour for lunch and finishes work at 16.30 hrs having completed his contracted daily attendance of seven hours.

Example 2   The following day, the same employee finds it convenient to start work at 09.15 hrs. He takes the fixed lunch break of one hour and finishes his contracted number of hours at 17.15 hrs.

Refinements of the Flexible Working Day

It is possible to elaborate on the basic concept of the flexible working day in such a way that the essential aim (which is to provide flexibility in starting and finishing times) is expanded to allow the employee greater control in the allocation of his working time.

REFINEMENT 1 THE LUNCH BREAK
Four types of lunch break can be identified.

21

Fixed Lunch Break

The period of time when a company stops work to enable its employees to rest and refresh themselves. Usually takes place approximately half-way through the working day.

For example from 13.00 hrs to 14.00 hrs *(See Fig.2.3.)*

Fig.2.3

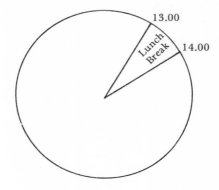

Staggered Lunch Break

Applies in certain situations when employees (or certain categories of employees) are required to stagger their lunch break to provide cover throughout the day, enabling continuity of job.

For example, on a telephone switchboard employing two telephonists:
Telephonist A Lunch Break 12.00 hrs to 13.00 hrs
Telephonist B Lunch Break 13.00 hrs to 14.00 hrs *(See Fig.2.4.)*

Fig.2.4

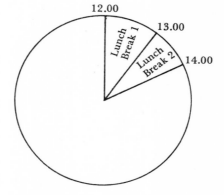

Flexible Lunch Break

A flexible time period, inserted between the two core times, during which the employee must take his lunch break. A minimum time period for lunch break will probably be prescribed by the company. Subject to this constraint the employee can decide the length of his lunch break and is free to take it at any time during the flexible lunch break. *(See Fig.2.5).*

Fig.2.5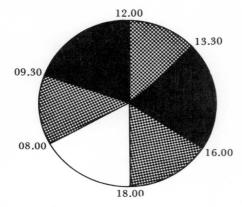

Example 3   The company has prescribed a minimum lunch period of ½ hour. An employee starts work at 09.30 hrs and breaks for lunch at 12.00 hrs. He resumes work at 13.00 hrs and, in order to work his daily contracted hours of seven, he finishes work at 17.30 hrs.

Semi-Flexible Lunch Break

A fixed close-down period when all employees stop work, with flexible time bands preceding and following this fixed period. The fixed period may, or may not, be equal in time to the minimum time period prescribed by the company.

Example 4   Fixed period is equal to prescribed minimum periods
(See Fig.   of ¾ hr. An employee starts work at 08.30 hrs. He
2.6)   takes his lunch break at 12.00 hrs, but cannot recommence work until 13.15 hrs, at the end of the fixed period. He then works until 16.45 hrs in order

23

to work his daily contracted hours of seven.

Fig.2.6

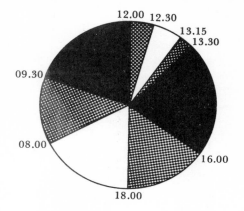

Example 5 Fixed period is less than the minimum period.
Fixed period is ½ hour
Minimum period is ¾ hour
(See Fig.2.7)
An employee starts work at 08.30 hrs and commences his lunch period at 12.30 hrs (the beginning of the fixed period). He cannot re-start until 13.15 hrs, 15 minutes after the end of the fixed period. He then works through until 16.15 hrs when he will have worked his seven daily contracted hours.

Fig.2.7

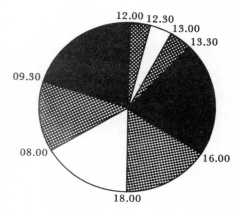

No problems regarding contravention of the minimum period are likely to arise when the fixed period is greater than the minimum period. This could only occur if the employee commenced work before the end of the fixed lunch period. Even in the event of this happening, he would not be able to count any time worked during this period towards his recorded hours of attendance (for definition of recorded hours see below). In general, the flexible or semi-flexible lunch break is extremely popular with employees. Some may do a little extra shopping or fit in a visit to the hairdresser. Others have found that for the first time they are able to go home for lunch to see their family. For those who take their meals in works canteens it probably means that they will be able to complete their lunch in a shorter period, go back to work more quickly and leave earlier in the evening.

The semi-flexible lunch break may be particularly helpful to companies who have a works canteen which is used extensively by the employees, in that, by nature of the flexibility either side of the stipulated closure, the workforce are likely to stagger the time of arrival at the canteen thus spreading the work load of the canteen staff. The disadvantage, from the company point of view is that, by introducing a third period of flexible time, the core time is being further reduced.

REFINEMENT 2 THE DEBIT/CREDIT BALANCE
So far we have considered only the most basic version of the flexible working hour system. Flexibility is built into the working day and the employee is expected to arrange his working hours in such a way that the daily hours worked under the new system are the same as the daily hours worked when the company operated a fixed working day (the daily contracted hours). If, because of a heavy workload, the employee exceeds the daily contracted hours under the new system, he cannot carry over his excess hours as credits. (He may, of course, be paid overtime, but this would necessitate pre-arrangement and permission from his superior).

Similarly, if, because of an urgent personal commitment, an employee has to leave work during the final flexible time period of the day *before* he has recorded his daily contracted hours, he must seek permission to do so and may, in some circumstances, suffer financial loss. The following example illustrates this.

Example 6 An employee gets a lift to work from a friend and is *(See Fig. 2.8)* available to start work at 08.30 hrs. At 17.30 hrs.

the end of the working day, his friend picks him up. Whilst it is permissible for him to work between these starting and finishing times if he so wishes, (thus recording 8 hours per day) his excess of 1 hour over the contracted day of 7 hours cannot be credited to him. He may, of course, start at 08.30 hrs and finish at 16.30 hrs but will inevitably find that he is killing time since, unless there is some specific appointment to be kept, there will be little he can do in this time.

Fig.2.8

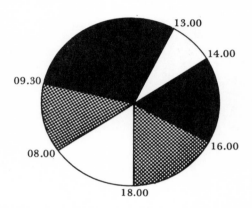

This type of flexible working has a number of disadvantages to the employee. Choice is severely limited where he is constrained by external factors. Nevertheless, the system is in operation in certain companies where the main aim has been to reduce the transport difficulties involved when large numbers of employees arrive and depart simultaneously on a fixed working day. By having a flexible or semi-flexible lunch hour, it also eases the situation when large numbers of employees go home for lunch.

It must be said, however, that if this is the limit to which the flexible working principle is to be developed, the choice available to employees will be only marginally greater than that given by a staggered hour system. By introducing a system of debits and credits the doors are opened to an entirely new approach to the structuring of the working week, the working month and the working year. The choices open to the employee are multiplied many-fold, yet the employer can retain control of the situation and ensure operational efficiency, by imposing certain constraints and limits.

Before this refinement is elaborated, some more definitions

are necessary.

Contracted Attendance Hours   The number of hours an employee is contracted to work in a given period. For example, if an employee has a contract which requires him to work a seven hour day (his contracted daily hours) then, if he is contracted to a five-day week, his contracted attendance hours are —
   35 hours per week
   140 hours per 4 week period

Recorded Hours   The number of hours an employee is in attendance (and is credited with attendance) at his place of employment.

Accounting Period   The period used by the company for the calculation of wages of employees. The accounting period may vary with classes of employees. Thus for clerical and administrative workers the accounting period is either one calendar month or four weeks. For hourly paid staff an accounting period of one week might be used. There are distinct advantages if all the accounting periods used for the various classes of employees are sub-multiples of the accounting year of fifty-two weeks.

Creation of a Credit   Occurs whenever an employee's recorded hours exceeds his contracted attendance hours at a given point in time.

Creation of a Debit   Occurs when an employee's recorded hours are less than his contracted attendance hours at a given point in time.

Settlement Period   The period during which recorded hours are accounted for, in a flexible working hour system. During this period, the general aim is that employee's recorded hours should be approximately equal to the contracted attendance hours for the same period (subject to any carry-over balance allowed).

Carry-over Balance   The number of debit or credit hours which an employee is allowed to carry forward from one settlement period to the next.

These concepts can be illustrated by the following examples of the use of credits, debits and balances.

Example of Flexible Working Day

A company has changed over from a fixed working day (*see Fig. 2.9*) in which:

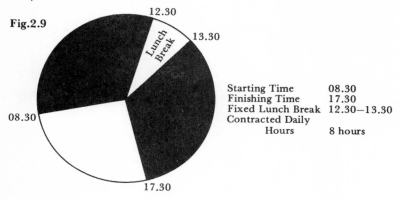

Fig.2.9

Starting Time	08.30
Finishing Time	17.30
Fixed Lunch Break	12.30–13.30
Contracted Daily Hours	8 hours

In adopting a flexible working day (*see Fig.2.10*) the company stipulates:

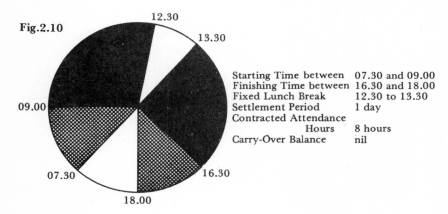

Fig.2.10

Starting Time between	07.30 and 09.00
Finishing Time between	16.30 and 18.00
Fixed Lunch Break	12.30 to 13.30
Settlement Period	1 day
Contracted Attendance Hours	8 hours
Carry-Over Balance	nil

This means, in effect, that at the end of each working day — recorded hours should equal contracted attendance hours.

From the employee's point of view this means that,

(i)   all debits created during the day must be worked out by 18.00 hrs.
(ii)   all credits created during the day and still in existence at 18.00 hrs are lost.

An employee commences work at 07.30 hrs and, allowing for the fixed lunch break, he has eight recorded hours by 16.30 hrs. If he works until 17.30 hrs he will have exceeded his contracted atten dance hours by 1 hour. Since he cannot carry this credit over from one day to the next, this credit is lost.

Example of Flexible Working Week

Using a day as settlement period imposes severe limitations on the development of the flexible working concept. By extending the settlement period to a week, and allowing a carry-over of debits and credits from one settlement period to the next, employees now have more flexibility to cope with fluctuating work loads, personal problems and other commitments. Once a carry-over balance has been defined, the employees main concern will be to ensure that —

(i)   he is always present during core time
(ii)   his carry-over balance from one period to the next does not exceed the stipulated allowance

A company operates a flexible working system *(See Fig.2.11)* in which:

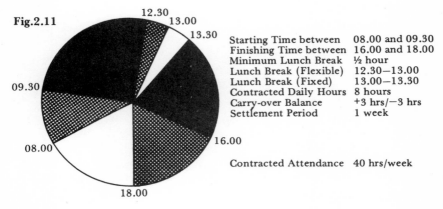

Fig.2.11

Starting Time between	08.00 and 09.30
Finishing Time between	16.00 and 18.00
Minimum Lunch Break	½ hour
Lunch Break (Flexible)	12.30—13.00
Lunch Break (Fixed)	13.00—13.30
Contracted Daily Hours	8 hours
Carry-over Balance	+3 hrs/—3 hrs
Settlement Period	1 week
Contracted Attendance	40 hrs/week

An employee completes the following recorded hours from Monday to Thursday.

Day	Start Work	Start Lunch	Finish Lunch	Finish Work	Day Credit/Debit	Cumulative Credit/Debit
Monday	08.00	13.00	13.30	17.30	+1	+1
Tuesday	09.00	13.00	13.30	16.30	−1	nil
Wednesday	09.30	12.30	13.30	16.00	−2½	−2½
Thursday	09.00	13.00	13.30	16.00	−1½	−4

Since the maximum carry-over balance is 3 hours (debit or credit) the employee must now organise his working day on Friday so that by 18.00 hrs on Friday evening, his debit is less than 3 hours. One way of doing this would be as follows

Friday	08.00	13.00	13.30	18.00	+1½	−2½

The debit balance of −2½ hrs is carried forward to the next week, as this is within the permissible limit. Note that, in working off his credit of one hour, which he accrued during work on Monday, he has had to take the time out of the flexible time bands in the working day. This constraint may, in fact, be stipulated by the company, but we will be examining this question of credit/debit utilisation in more detail under credit and debit leaves.

EXAMPLE OF FLEXIBLE WORKING MONTH

There are certain advantages in extending the settlement period to a calendar month or four week period. More flexibility is available for both employer and employees and, if a larger carry-over balance is used, companies generally find that this is welcomed by staff and does not necessarily raise problems for the organisation. There may be fears that, since no limit on debits/credits is imposed *during* the settlement periods, some employees might act irresponsibly and amass very large debits which they would then find it impossible to work off during the latter part of the period. This is always a possibility, but experience indicates that the overwhelming majority of employees quickly appreciate the mechanics of debit/credit carry-over balances and rarely find themselves in an impossible position with regard to balances at the end of a settlement period.

To conclude on Refinement 2, in which the basic principle of flexible working has been opened up to include the possibility of debit/credit carry-over balance at the end of settlement periods, it is worth noting that the evidence available indicates that a month is the most popular settlement period.

REFINEMENT 3 CREDIT AND DEBIT LEAVES
So far we have assumed that, when permissible credits or debits are carried over to the next settlement period, they can only be 'worked off' during the flexible time bands of the working day.

Credit Leave Units

In the case of a credit balance, it may be possible to extend employee choice by allowing the employee to take time off in half-day units or whole-day units. This type of credit leave would only be granted subject to certain requirements which could include that —

  (i)   the needs of the job are met;
 (ii)   the absence is approved by the supervisor
(iii)   the work of the section/department does not suffer
(iv)   the total number of credit leave units taken in a settlement period does not exceed a certain, pre-determined total.

Some firms have found it necessary to define a half-day or full-day credit unit in terms of recorded hours and, although this appears unnecessary, and imposes a possible limitation in at least one case, it appears to operate fairly universally in flexible working hour schemes.

This definitive approach to Credit Leave is based on the following propositions —

1. Where Credit Leave Unit = 1 Full Working Day
then, 1 Credit Leave Unit = Average Number of Contracted Daily Hours. Thus if an organisation operating a five day week requires a contracted attendance of 140 hours per 4 week period then,

$$1 \text{ Credit Leave Unit} = \frac{140}{4 \times 5} = 7 \text{ Debit Hours}$$

2. Where Credit Leave Unit = ½ Working Day

31

then 1 Credit Leave Unit =
$$\left(\frac{\text{Average No of Contracted Daily Hours}}{2} \right)$$

thus, if an organisation operating a *four* * day week requires a contracted attendance of 144 hrs per 4 week period then,

$$1 \text{ Credit Leave Unit} = \left(\frac{144}{4 \times 4 \times 2} \right) = 4\frac{1}{2} \text{ Debit Hours}$$

Example of Credit Leave

An organisation operates a flexible working hour system *(See Fig. 2.12)* on a five day week.

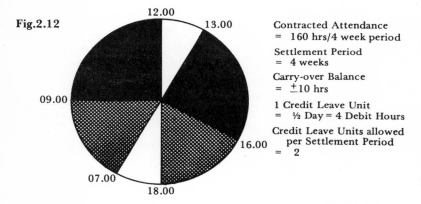

Fig.2.12

Contracted Attendance
= 160 hrs/4 week period

Settlement Period
= 4 weeks

Carry-over Balance
= ±10 hrs

1 Credit Leave Unit
= ½ Day = 4 Debit Hours

Credit Leave Units allowed
per Settlement Period
= 2

Consider an employee who, at the end of, say, settlement period 1 has 170 recorded hours (against his contracted attendance hours of 160) and carries over 10 hours of credit to the start of settlement period 2. He arranges to take the morning off on Day 1 of settlement period 2.

He works from 13.00 hrs (the soonest he can start work after the fixed lunch break) until 18.00 hrs and this gives him 5 recorded hours of attendance, and this, when balanced against the contracted half-day of 4 hours, gives him a credit of 1 hour.

His 'bank balance' of debits/credits will change as follows between 07.00 hrs on Day 1 and 07.00 hrs on Day 2.

---

* The authors have no knowledge of any organisation operating a fwh scheme on a 4 day week. This is taken for illustration only.

Table 2.1. Adjustments for Settlement Period 2

		Cumulated Debits-Credits
Day 1	07.00 hrs Carry-Over Balance from Period 1	+10
	13.00 hrs Credit Leave Unit	−4
	18.00 hrs Daily Balance (recorded—contracted) hours (5 − 4)	+1
Day 2	07.00 hrs Brought Forward	+7

Debit Leave Units

More flexibility can be obtained, and much employee good-will generated, if the company decide that, even if they are not actually in credit, employees may take leave units, provided that the general requirements for credit leave units are met *(see page 31)*. Additional requirements might be that —

(i) the section-manager's permission is also required
(ii) the taking of such debit leave should not result in the employee exceeding, at that point in time, the negative carry-over balance allowed at the end of a settlement period.

Example of Debit Leave

Using the flexible working hour structure of the previous example *(see page 32)* consider an employee who, at the end of day 3, in say, settlement period 5, has a cumulative debit-credit balance of −3 hours. He applies for permission to take the afternoon off on day 4, and his section-manager grants this as he is satisfied that —

(a) job and section requirements can be met
(b) the employee's total of leave units for this settlement period will not exceed 2.
(c) the employee's 'bank balance' at the end of day 4 will not exceed −10 hrs.

On day 4 the employee works from 07.30 hrs until 12.00 hrs, and during the day his 'bank balance' changes as follows.

Table 2.2. Adjustments for Settlement Period 5

		Cumulated Debits-Credits
Day 4	07.00 hrs Brought forward from day 3	−3
	13.00 hrs (recorded−contracted) hrs =	
	(4½−4)hrs	+½
	18.00 hrs Debit Leave Unit	−4
Day 5	07.00 hrs Brought forward from day 4	−6½

Had the employee's 'bank balance' been −7 at the end of day 3, the section manager might have granted permission, only on condition that the employee worked from 07.00 hrs until 12.00 hrs on day 4, thus ensuring that the nett balance of debits-credits did not exceed −10 at the end of the day. The reader might like to check, for himself, that the balance would, in fact, be −10 hours.

The 'Declared' Credit-Debit Leave Unit

There may be occasions when it would be a convenience to the organisation (and, in certain cases, to the employees) if a complete 'shutdown' could be operated, without inflicting a financial burden on the staff through loss of wages and salary. Such a situation could arise where, say, a single working day fell between a normal weekend rest-day and a public holiday. For example, where Christmas Day falls on Tuesday, it would be convenient for company and staff to have Christmas Eve (Monday) as a free day. Under a flexible working hour system the organisation might decide to 'declare' a compulsory full day's leave. The contracted hours lost would be 'charged' against each employee's cumulated credit-debit balance so that no wages were lost. It might be necessary to waive the requirement regarding the total number of credit leaves per month and the maximum negative carry-over balance allowed per settlement period, but, providing such a procedure has been discussed and approved by the employees, it provides an interesting adaptation of the credit-debit leave refinement.

One can distinguish other situations where a 'declared leave' would have the support of the employees and could be to the operational benefit of the organisation. For example, in firms subject to very short-cycle variations in trade, an adaptation of the above system might be used to stabilise the wages of employees during 'slack' periods. The debits accrued could be worked off during busy periods. Obviously, the employees (and unions where applicable) would have to be fully consulted, but it is difficult to see what objections would be raised to proposals designed to protect staff from wide fluctuations in earnings.

'Ad Hoc' Leave in Core Time

If a debit-credit leave scheme is incorporated in a flexible working hour system there is an implicit acceptance by senior management that core time is not sacrosanct; that is to say, the organisation is accepting that, in certain circumstances, their employees can be absent during those parts of the working day when attendance is normally mandatory. A logical extension of this thinking is to allow employees to take time off (other than complete leave units) during core time.

It would, of course, have to be stressed that ad hoc absences in core time would only be permissible in cases of urgent personal need. It cannot be over-emphasised that, unless all employees clearly appreciate the importance of mandatory attendance in core time, flexible working cannot possibly meet the needs of the organisation. Thus, where ad hoc absences of this type are permissible, there is a heavy responsibility on all supervisors to ensure that this concession is not abused.

Having sounded the appropriate warnings, it must be said that this facility can generate a tremendous amount of good will among employees and there is little evidence that, where made available, the concession is abused.

Constraints on Flexible Working

Having refined the system, it is now necessary to discuss three important aspects of flexible working which form constraints and have to be considered before we can develop a fwh scheme.

CONSTRAINT 1 FLEXIBLE TIME AND NEEDS OF THE ENTERPRISE
The impression given so far may appear to be one of unlimited choice for the employee during flexible times and limited choice during core time. Enough has been said about the latter to indicate that, while it is not inviolable, time-off during core time is regulated by a system of rules (See credit, debit, and ad hoc leaves,

35

pages 31—35).

So far, however, there has been no mention of rules for time off during flexible time, yet it must be apparent to the reader that where employees working on a flexible hour system have work tasks which integrate with the work tasks of colleagues, complete freedom of choice will not be possible, even in flexible time. Examples come easily to hand:

(i)   the production worker on an assembly line
(ii) the canteen assistant in the company canteen
(iii) the secretary and her boss
(iv) the office cleaners and the security men
      and so on.

This area will be explored more thoroughly in Chapter 5 for there are factors other than overlapping of work tasks which impose limitations on freedom of choice in flexible time. At this stage, it is enough to draw attention to the problem, so that it is recognized clearly that complete freedom of choice rarely exists. The needs of the organization must be met, if it is to remain viable.

Having made this point clear, there is a great deal of evidence which suggests that, provided this issue is openly discussed with employees there is a high level of acceptance and that in general, attitudes towards time off in flexible time are responsible and realistic.

CONSTRAINT 2 OVERTIME WORKING

It must be said at the outset that this is a potentially volatile area, unless management are prepared to think clearly about the issues involved, make decisions (possibly in consultation with the employees), and specify a precise body of rules which will define all aspects of overtime working. The problem arises because, unlike the fixed working day, the flexible working day has no precise boundaries of 'start' and 'finish' . With a fixed working day, any authorised work outside those boundaries is paid for at the appropriate rates. With flexible working, on the other hand, there are no such universal boundaries. Individual employees are permitted to create their own.

Thus, in approaching the question of overtime, management are generally presented with a wide number of choices, both as to

(i)   what will constitute overtime working

  (ii) what methods of recompense are to be available

 (iii) what discretion is to be granted to the employee in respect of the above.

It is possible to proceed by listing the choices available under the above headings.

  (i) Time worked will only be classed as overtime where
- (a) it takes place outside the bandwidth
- (b) it is in excess of the daily contracted hours on any day
- (c) it is in excess of the contracted attendance hours per settlement period in any settlement period.
- (d) it is in excess of the sum of the contracted attendance hours as in (c) above and the maximum credit hours allowed for that settlement period.
- (e) it involves the employee in arriving before, or staying after, the times at which he would normally start or finish work.
- (f) it is authorised by a superior
- (g) it is authorised, in advance, by a superior

 (ii) Time classed as overtime will
- (a) be paid for at the appropriate overtime rates,
- (b) be added, as credits, to the employee's normal cumulated credit-debit balance, for the settlement period.
- (c) be deposited, as credits, in a 'special credit balance' from which credit leave units may be taken

(iii) Where options with regard to method exist as in (ii) above, then
- (a) choice of option will be at the election of the employee and/or the discretion of the employer
- (b) where options (b) and/or (c) are adopted, the credits will be suitably time-increased to take account of the appropriate overtime rates
- (c) where option (b) is exercised, the employee may/may not take credit leave in excess of the normal maximum specified under the flexible working hour scheme
- (d) where option (c) is adopted, credit leave taken out of the special credit balance will/will not be subject to an agreed maximum and will/will not be considered separately from any maximum specified under the flexible

working scheme.

The choices listed above are not necessarily mutually exclusive, and the number of combinations possible are very large indeed. This should indicate the care which must be given to this question. A superficial approach will only lead to problems, both with the employees and their unions.

The above is best illustrated by an example: The German firm Messerschmidt GmbH has the following arrangements with respect to overtime working:

Classification of Overtime   Where an employee works beyond the time he would normally start or finish *and* that work is at the request of a superior, that time is classed as overtime. (That is, only conditions (i)(e) and (i)(g) above must be satisfied, but they must both be satisfied.)

Remuneration of Overtime   Overtime will be paid at the appropriate overtime rate or the employee can take time off in lieu. *(See (ii)(a), and (ii)(b), above.)* choice of method is at the discretion of the employee [(iii)(a)] and credit time is suitably increased to take account of overtime rates [(iii)(b)]. Other arrangements for overtime are shown in Appendix I.

CONSTRAINT 3 TIME RECORDING

An essential requirement in the operation of a flexible working hour scheme is an objective time recording system. The function of such a system is not to control punctuality, but to provide each individual, and his employer, with a factual record of the actual hours he has worked during any settlement period. To be really effective, it should provide him with such a record at *any* point in time, during such a period.

Innocuous as such an aim may be, the main opposition to flexible working hours has usually centred round the need to introduce, re-introduce or continue with formal time recording. If the greatest resistance has been mounted by office staff, one can only assume that this is because the introduction of time recording is seen as a loss of status. Yet opposition must be expected from all sections of an organisation. Where change is concerned, even those employees who have 'clocked-on' for years can be expected to produce the most unexpected and stubborn resistance to it.

The whole question of time recording is explored in Chapter 4.

But it is worth noting at this stage that there are four basic alternatives available —

(i) Manual Recording: employees themselves complete their time attendance directly on time sheets or on a register/ day card system from where attendance hours are transferred to time sheets directly or via a computer process.
(ii) Time Clock: some manufacturers of traditional time clocks have adapted their equipment for recording attendance hours; other companies have carried out their own adaptions to suit the requirements of their flexible working scheme.
(iii) Meters: each employee has a personal recording unit which 'meters' his total hours of attendance accumulating and shows the employee (and his employer) how his current account of hours stands. at any point in time. The meter is not unlike a car mileometer in method of operation.
(iv) Computers: Computerised badge and key readers. Each employee has his own personalised plastic badge which he inserts into a terminal to record attendance. The terminals are connected to a control unit which prepares the required information in a form compatible with a computer input requirement.

CONSTRAINT 4 ABSENCES FROM THE WORK PLACE

In addition to absences of the type covered by credit-debit leaves and *ad hoc* leaves, absences from the work place (covering core-time and/or flexible time) will take place from time to time. The reasons for these absences will be many and varied, but they will largely fall into two categories.

(i) *Absences on company business*
It is essential that provision be made to ensure that, while absent from his place of work on the company's business, the employee is credited with attendance hours. This means that the system of time recording is programmed to take account of official absences of this type and to record an appropriate amount of hours.
(ii) *Other absences*
These will arise during illness, urgent personal business, holidays, for attendance at weddings, funerals and for visits to doctors and dentists. There are two questions to be resolved here. Which type of 'other absence' is to qualify for inclusion

as attendance at the work place and how is the recording system to be programmed to cope with such absences.

Lest it be imagined that these absences constitute a minor problem, it is necessary to appreciate that the system must cope with an absence from work which might have multiple causes, Consider the employee who, while engaged in company business in another town, has a minor car accident which results in him not reaching his home until 2 am the next morning, keeps him in bed for two days and, even when fit, because of the damage to his car, he can only report for work at 10 am on his first day back (one hour after the start of core time). He has then to leave at 2 pm to attend the out-patients department at the local hospital.

Like time-recording, absences from work other than leave units can introduce many problems and it is well to note the potential difficulties at this stage. The problems will be explored in depth when we consider this area in Chapter 5.

3. Advantages & Disadvantages of Flexible Working Hours

In putting forward the claimed advantages and disadvantages with f.w.h. the authors question the validity of carrying out a balancing operation where not only is the weight given to individual pros and cons indeterminate, but in some cases, their very existence may be doubted. However, if the lists which follow are used constructively, then they should be seen clearly for what they are, that is, generalised, often highly speculative, claims or counter-claims advanced by a range of interested parties for a variety of reasons. Looked on in this way they can provide a useful lead into the pre-evaluation stage of a company exploratory model. It is with this in mind that the authors advance the following summary of pros and cons for management, employees, customers and society generally. We do not claim that this list is exhaustive, nor that any one advantage or disadvantage would apply or not apply in any particular organisation.

Management Attitudes

It can be argued that most of the advantages for management will be indirect, that is that the improvements at the "human relations" level (morale, motivation) will indirectly improve company performance. On the other hand, there are those who claim that direct economic advantages accrue through better use of capital assets, better workflow, rhythm etc. But evidence suggests that the two types of benefit tend to overlap.

   (i)   *A more responsible attitude to work by the workforce*
      (a)   Employees come to work to do a job rather than to work 'n' hours per day. Jobs in hand tend to be finished: for example a typist will stay on to finish letters knowing that she will be credited with the time equivalent.
      (b)   Encourages a team spirit (particularly on group work) where individuals have to consult each other before

           making a group decision about starting and finishing times.

(c)   The "excuse" for lateness or absence from work on personal business is unnecessary.

(d)   Employees are now prepared to identify the peaks and troughs in their workloads since attendance time can be individually adjusted to suit.

(ii) *More effective work performance by workforce*

(a)   Reduction in number of days lost through *alleged* illness.

(b)   Reduction in costs for a given output, through a more highly motivated work force and the need for less overtime working.

(c)   Casual gossip at the beginning and end of each day tends to be reduced with employees arriving in a random manner and quietly settling down to work.

(d)   For office staff the creation of a quiet time (outside core time) can lead to more effective work output.

(iii) *Organisational improvements*

(a)   The necessity for more precise instructions to subordinates leads to an improvement in communications.

(b)   Better utilisation of capital assets due to the longer band width than with the fixed working day.

(iv) *Attraction to labour*

(a)   Reduction in labour turnover is likely on the grounds that employees, being conditioned to a fwh scheme are less likely to be attracted to firms not operating such a scheme. This leads to a reduction in recruitment and training costs.

(b)   Where women have to be recruited fwh is a special incentive in terms of shopping, getting children to school, etc.

Management Disadvantages

(i) *Additional costs (time recording)*

Existing time recording equipment may need to be modified or new systems will have to be installed and tested. The costs will vary according to the type of equipment used, but it is a distinct aspect of fwh systems which can weight heavily on the debit side. Once installed maintenance and running costs will have to be met.

(ii) *Administration costs*
   (a) The cost of resources for development and installation (project leader, steering committee, etc.).
   (b) Once installed the system must be administered. In particular, where the hours worked by employees are reconciled centrally, the clerical cost entailed may be considerable if the fwh system cannot be integrated into existing procedures.

(iii) *Overheads*
   (a) Since heat, light and power will be required at the extremities of the bandwidth an additional cost will have to be carried.
   (b) Service and supervisory cover at extremes of bandwidth may be increased.
   (c) A larger car park may be required since, where previously employees may have shared transport, under fwh they tend to travel individually so that they can vary their hours to suit their own convenience.

(iv) *Operational inconvenience*
   (a) Employees may not be present when required. They are bound to regard the flexible bands as time periods during which they can exercise choice and management would be unwise to attempt an unreasonable restriction of this.
   (b) Supervision may be more difficult and responsibility will often need to be delegated to lower levels during the flexible bands. Additional work is posed for supervision in terms of controlling the fwh system.
   (c) Internal and external communications may deteriorate, since the guaranteed availability time is reduced to core time.

(v) *Safety and security*
   (a) Maintenance of security is more difficult when staff arrive and leave over a much wider period. Also, since employees are more likely to be working alone at the

extremities of the bandwidth, there is a security risk (for example, access to confidential information) and theft risks increase.
   (b)   In work technology where safety hazards exist, certain tasks may have to be limited to core time (for example, experiments in a chemical development laboratory).
   (c)   Hazards could arise if workers are involved in their work tasks for too long a period.

(vi) *Miscellaneous*
   (a)   Staff may deliberately build up credit time by 'staying over' for a greater period than the job demands.
   (b)   Friction may develop between employees who have the freedom of choice of working hours and those who are excluded or restricted because of the job they do.

Employee Advantages

Obviously many of the employer advantages also carry advantage to the employee. Those claimed for the workforce are as follows —

  (i) *Better balance between private life and work*
   (a)   Lateness and resulting 'guilt' complexes disappear.
   (b)   Shopping requirements, getting children to school and similar domestic activities can be accommodated.
   (c)   Personal embarrassment is avoided since it is no longer necessary to disclose private affairs before making a planned absence.
   (d)   When credit time can be taken in half day or whole day units, relaxation and leisure time pursuits expand.

 (ii) *Reduced stress*
   (a)   Individuals vary in their physiological and psychological make-up and a system of fwh allows some degree of adjustment to these body rhythms.
   (b)   The tensions both physical and mental, associated with rush hour travel are reduced.

(iii) *Economic advantages*
   (a)   Travelling costs may be reduced through off-peak travel and by shared transport with family/relations or friends

at times convenient to them.
(b) Lateness and financial penalties disappear.
(c) Many employees have always expected to work additional time, where necessary, without extra pay. With fwh additional time worked is credited.

Employee Disadvantages

(i) *Economic*
  (a) Because of better matching of work time to workload, in some schemes overtime earnings may be reduced.
  (b) Where productivity rises or there is a better use of capital assets, the employees may not share the benefits.
  (c) 'Personal absence' privileges (visit to the doctor or dentist) may be lost.

(ii) *Working conditions*
  (a) Time recording may be necessary for employees who have never had to use such a system before.
  (b) Levels of supervision and services may not be available at the extremities of bandwidth.

Customer Advantages

(i) Increased hours of contact with an organisation is possible since the bandwidth is greater than the replaced fixed working day.
(ii) Core time establishes a more definitive period within which contact can be made with individuals in the organisation.

Customer Disadvantages

(i) Possible restrictions on times when delivery/collection of goods is possible.
(ii) Contact with the public may be restricted to core time only.
(iii) Time span, during which specific individuals can be contacted with any degree of certainty, is reduced.

Benefits to Society

If there are disadvantages for society in general, they are not immediately obvious. In fact, it seems likely that if the benefits claimed (see below) do materialise then society itself will exert pressures on organisations to adopt fwh schemes.

  (i) Reduced pressure on transport services, particularly during rush hour periods.

 (ii) Reduced load on hospital services. This will follow if as has been argued in 'Employee Advantages' (ii) above, the physical ailments and neuroses of modern industrial society are reduced by the impact of fwh on work and travel systems.

(iii) More employment in the leisure industry through the creation of a work week structure which encourages more leisure time pursuits.

(iv) Spreading of load on health and social services. There will be less strain on doctors, dentists, etc, to provide services outside the working day.

4. Time Recording

The Need to Record Attendance Time

A basic requirement of flexible working hour systems is the need to record attendance time. This is necessary in order to ensure that:

(i) employees are working within the limits of the scheme; that is, the contracted number of hours per settlement period.
(ii) legal and other regulations governing employee's working hours are adhered to.
(iii) the organisation, and its employees, can calculate debit/credit balances for each individual, at any point in time, during a settlement period.

Comparison with traditional time recording
It is important that the differences between traditional time recording ('clocking in' and 'clocking out') and the system of attendance recording associated with flexible working time be fully understood.

Traditional time recording is used
(i) to control punctuality by recording each individual's arrival time and finishing time.
(ii) as a means of assessing each individual's attendance time so that remuneration at standard rates and overtime rates can be computed.

This emphasis on the recording of actual starting and finishing times is, of course, a fundamental feature of the fixed working day, but it has no significance at all in the flexible working day. Thus time recording systems used in fwh systems are concerned with recording actual hours of attendance, rather than absolute starting and finishing times. These systems are more concerned with 'metering' than with 'clocking'.

The fact that some of the methods used embody clocks (or clock times) does not detract from this fundamental difference. Since the concept of 'arriving late' or 'leaving early' is no longer valid, 'clock times' lose their old significance. Absolute times may be needed to compute overtime rates, but where this is necessary a separate recording system for overtime worked will normally be used.

Resistance to time recording

For many employees, the concept of time recording will, initially, be unacceptable. At the same time, the intensity of rejection will obviously be related to the type of recording used, and this is discussed below. What must be faced is that, if a flexible working hour scheme is to operate successfully, a control system of some type will be necessary. This in no way imputes the honesty of employees. In fact, one of the systems used (the manual) depends greatly, for its success, on the basic honesty of those using it.

What is important is that resistance to time-recording must be overcome and a method of recording attendance introduced. Hopefully, there is a great deal of evidence that where fwh has been applied, employees who have not previously been used to recording their hours worked have generally accepted the need for a formal method. However, this can be a point of dissension and should be carefully considered when deciding which type of recording system to adopt. The matter of selling a system to the employees is discussed in detail in Chapter 6.

Methods of time recording

There are, of course, several ways of recording time and these were briefly mentioned in Chapter 2. They are *manual recording, time clocks, meters* and *computerised systems* and these are expanded below.

Manual Systems

Some organisations are using manual systems with success. Others have used them for a trial period only and have later decided to change to objective recording, using some form of electrical or mechanical equipment. One large British company operated a manual system during its pilot scheme whereby employees signed on in the morning and off at the end of the working day in the register provided. The information thus recorded was punched on to computer clock cards and a weekly tabulation was produced for each section, showing the total hours worked and the debit and credit balance for each employee. There are many types of manual recording systems available and three examples are given:

(a) *Example I (See Figure 4.1)*
This is the simplest form of a monthly time sheet, designed for an employee working Monday to Friday on a fwh system incorporating a flexible lunch period. The employee completes columns 'a' to 'd' daily as they occur and at the end of the week completes the column 'e' "daily mins. worked". Before leaving work on Friday (or at the end of the working week) a calculation is made of the total hours worked and this is compared with the contracted hours. The weekly debit/ credit position is then calculated and entered in column 'f'. Finally, taking into account any balance brought forward,the appropriate credit or debit balance is entered in column 'g'. At the end of the settlement period, (in the examples shown either four or five week periods) the employee completes the card, enters his opening credit or debit balance on his next months card, signs it and passes it to his departmental head for approval.

Note: On this card there is no way of recording absences.

(b) *Example II (See Figure 4.2)*
A diary sheet for manually recording flexible working hours but having the following refinements over example I.
  (i) *Reasons for absence*
  Column 'a' Reason: enables an employee to record a reason for being away from his place of work e.g. sickness, holiday.
  (ii) *Recording of overtime at varying rates*
  An employee can record total hours worked in column 'c' and extend this to columns 'd' and 'e' for allocation of time worked to flexible working or overtime, the latter being split between varying rates. (The manner in which overtime and overtime rates has been computed need not concern us here).
  (iii) *Pay instructions*
  Column 'f' is designed for a departmental head to analyse hours worked as an instruction for payment of wages.
  The abbreviations shown are:

Fig. 4.1 : Manual Time Recording

DEPT. *Personnel*		NAME *J. miller*			EMPLOYEE NUMBER *282*		

SETTLEMENT PERIOD	FROM w/c 5ᵗʰ Feb.		TO w/c 26ᵗʰ Feb.	CONTRACTED HOURS 4 wks x 37.5 hrs = 150		BALANCE B/F	+2.00

WEEK NO	DAY	START A.M	FINISH A.M	START PM	FINISH PM	DAILY MINUTES WORKED	WEEKLY HRS MINS	PERIOD HRS MINS
1	MON	9.00	12.32	1.30	4.30	392		
	TUES.	9.20	12.50	1.32	4.30	388	35.45	+0.15
	WED.	9.05	1.00	1.35	5.05	445		
	THUR.	8.30	12.40	1.30	5.00	460	-1.45	
	FRI.	8.50	12.45	1.45	5.30	460		
2	MON							
	TUES.							
	WED							
	THUR							
	FRI							
3	MON							
	TUES							
	WED							
	THUR.							
	FRI							
4	MON							
	TUES							
	WED							
	THUR							
	FRI.							
5	MON							
	TUES.							
	WED							
	THUR							
	FRI.							
		(a)	(b)	(c)	(d)	(e)	(f)	(g)

EMPLOYEE SIGNATURE		APPROVED BY	
		DATE	

Fig 4.2 : Manual Recording

NAME ......*T. Hunt*...................   4 or 5 WEEK PERIOD ENDING ...*16 . 3 . 1973*......

		START & FINISHING TIME				TOTAL TIME	FLEXTIME	OVERTIME			PAY INSTRUCTIONS					DEPT. MANAGER INITIAL
DAY	REASON	A.M.		P.M.		HRS / 100	HRS / 100	1¼	1½	2	HOL TAP	SP	SNP	TAP	ANP	(Work)
		FROM	TO	FROM	TO											
WEEK 1 M		9.00	12.32	1.30	4.30	6 53	6 53									
Tu		9.00	12.50	1.30	5.00	9 33	7 33	2.00								
W	Sick leave					7 50	7 50					7.50				
Th		8.30	12.42	1.30	5.00	4 67	4 17	.50								J.C.M
F		9.05	12.30	1.30	6.00	9 92	6 92	3.00								
Sat																
Sun		9.00	12.0			3 00				3.00						
WEEK 2 M	absent - no pay					7 50	7 50								7.5	
Tu																
W																
Th																
F																
Sat																
Sun																
WEEK 3 M																
Tu																
W																
Th																
F																
Sat																
Sun																
WEEK 4 M																
Tu																
W																
Th																
F																
Sat																
Sun																
WEEK 5 M																
Tu																
W																
Th																
F																
Sat																
Sun																

KEY PAY INSTRUCTIONS

HOL TAP	HOLIDAY - TIME ALLOWED F/B
S.P	SICK PAY
S.N.P	SICK NO PAY
T.A.P	ABSENT - TIME ALLOWED F/B
A.N.P	ABSENT - NO PAY

A	TOTAL TIME
B	CREDITS/DEBITS LAST MONTH
C	TOTAL CREDITS (A + B)
D	TOTAL CONTRACTED HRS.
E	CREDITS/DEBITS C/F NEXT MONTH (D - C)

SIGNED ....

AUTHORISED BY ....

DEPT. MANAGER 67

HOL TAP — Holiday pay — time allowed paid
SP — Absence through sickness with pay
SNP — Absence through sickness — no pay
TAP — Time allowed paid
ANP — Absent no pay

For example: When the employee is on holiday for a whole day the number of hours of a standard day is entered in column HOL TAP (Holiday-time allowed paid). For an employee who is absent through illness for a whole day and requires payment for the day, an entry of the number of hours in a standard day is entered in column SP (sick pay). For an employee who is absent through illness for a whole day, but who will not receive a payment, an entry of the number of hours in a standard day is entered in column SNP (sick no pay).

(c) *Example III (See Figure 4.3)*

A register designed to record the arrival and finishing times of fwh. In some cases organisations insist that employees state their proposed times for starting and finishing work in advance. This applies to many types of team working but is particularly the case in manufacturing situations. For example, where a group of employees work on a conveyor line it will be necessary for the team to agree in advance the hours they will work and inform their supervisor accordingly. To allow for this facility to be recorded in writing the team enters its proposed starting and finishing times in advance of each day or week, dependant upon the requirement of supervision, and enters the actual times as they occur.

Advantages of a manual system
 (i) Initial equipment cost is negligible.
 (ii) The system may be viewed as the most progressive from a human relations aspect, in its recognition of the innate honesty and responsibility of all employees.

Disadvantages of a manual system
 (i) Administration costs may be high to fulfil information required.
 (ii) There is no visual indication as to an employee's presence on or absence from the premises.
 (iii) The system can cause friction within departments and between individuals. Although there is a basic assumption that the

Fig 4.3 : Manual Recording for Team Working

TEAM NO. 2	SUPERVISORS NAME John Jones	WEEK ENDING 16 · 3 · 1973

NAME		MON			TUES			WED.			THUR			FRI			TOTAL HOURS			
		S	L	F	S	L	F	S	L	F	S	L	F	S	L	F	WORKED	CONTRACTED	CREDIT B/F	CIF
J. JONES	PROP.	8·00	12·00 1·00	5·00	8·00	1·00	5·00	7·45	12·30 1·30	5·15	1·00	12·30 1·30	5·00	8·00	12·45 1·30	4·45				
	ACTUAL	8·00	12·00 1·00	5·00	8·00	12·00 1·00	5·00	7·45	12·30 1·30	5·15	8·00	12·30 1·30	5·00	8·00	12·45 1·30	4·45	40½	40	+2	-2½
A. BEST	PROP.																			
	ACTUAL																			
R. CORNISH.	PROP.																			
	ACTUAL																			
	PROP.																			
	ACTUAL																			
	PROP.																			
	ACTUAL																			
	PROP.																			
	ACTUAL																			
	PROP.																			
	ACTUAL																			
	PROP.																			
	ACTUAL																			
	PROP.																			
	ACTUAL																			
	PROP.																			
	ACTUAL																			

KEY

S	START
L	LUNCH
F	FINISH.

SUPERVISORS SIGNATURE	
APPROVED BY	
DATE	

company trusts each individual employee, experience indicates that individuals may not trust each other.

Time Clock Card Recording

Several manufacturers of conventional time clocks have adapted their equipment to allow for the recording of flexible working hours. Two examples are given below:

(a) *Example 1 — Clock card with direct subtraction recording — Fig. 4.4.*
The starting and finishing times, together with the recorded starting and finishing times of the mid-day break are recorded by the time clock against the appropriate space. Two points should be noted: (i) the days of the week progress from left to right and (ii) the time is being recorded vertically each day, starting at the bottom of the card with 'Flexible Start'. In the example Miss Smith worked on Monday from 9.00 am to 13.00 and from 14.00 to 16.30. (The recorder has the facility of recording to 1/10th of an hour, i.e. six minute periods. If required the recorder can be fitted with a device to record to 1/20th of an hour i.e. three minute periods). At the end of the week working hours are calculated and entered at the top of the card.
It can be seen that Miss Smith worked 34.4 hours during the week, against a contracted attendance of 37.00 hours giving a debit of 2.6 hours for the week. The example shown in Figure 4.4 is known as 'Selectime' and is marketed by International Time Recording Co. Ltd. (with whose permission this facsimile is reproduced).

(b) *Example II — Clock card with line difference (Fig. 4.5)*
The clock card is punched by the employee in the normal way. The flexible working parts of the day are broken down into 15 minute units and the recording is based upon a 'swings and roundabouts' experience which has proved to be precise enough for this purpose.
In the example both the AM and PM flexible bands are each of two hours split into equal parts of 15 mins. AM Flexible time is from 08.00 hours to 10.00 hours and PM Flexible time from 16.30 to 18.30 hours. The starting time

Fig 4.4 : Time Clock Card with Direct Subtraction Recording

iTR selectime RECORD

REF _____ No. 134 _____

W/ENDING _____ 9/12/72 _____

NAME _____ MISS A. SMITH _____

37 0	STANDARD HOURS	
34.4	ACTUAL HOURS	

DIFFERENCE	2.6	✗	—
B/F FROM PREVIOUS PERIOD		+	—
C/F TO NEXT PERIOD	2.6	✗	—

MO	TU	WE	TH	FR	
ᴹᴼ16.5		ᵂᴱ17.0	ᵀᴴ17.5	ᶠᴿ18.0	FLEXIBLE FINISH
	ᵀᵁ16.0				CORE
ᴹᴼ14.0	ᵀᵁ13.5	ᵂᴱ13.5	ᵀᴴ13.0	ᶠᴿ14.0	(LUNCH)
ᴹᴼ13.0	ᵀᵁ12.0	ᵂᴱ12.0	ᵀᴴ12.0	ᶠᴿ13.0	
				ᶠᴿ10.0	CORE
ᴹᴼ9.0	ᵀᵁ8.5	ᵂᴱ8.0	ᵀᴴ9.1		FLEXIBLE START
4.0	3.5	4.0	2.9	3.0	17.4 (A.M. TOTAL)
2.5	2.5	3.5	4.5	4.0	17.0 (P.M. TOTAL)
6.5	6.0	7.5	7.4	7.0	34.4 TOTAL

LS 4772

Fig 4.5 : Time Clock Card with Line Difference

NAME J. Orton	113	CONTRACTED HRS	37½
DEPT Personnel		CREDIT H.P.S.	½
WEEK ENDING 16-3-1973		DEBIT HRS.	

	1	2	3	4	5	6	7	TOTAL
AM FLEX BAND 8ºº–10ºº 1	S 8 00				L 8.08			
2								
3		≥ 8 32		F 8.36				
4								
5								
6			Z 9.18					
7								
8								
PM FLEX BAND 16³⁰–18³⁰ 1	Σ 16.30							
2					L 16.48			
3								
4			Z 17.25	F 17.27				
5		≥ 17.40						
6								
7								
8								
+		2	-	1	1			4
-		-	2	-	-			2

is stamped above, and the finishing time below the centre of the card. The days of the week are from left to right. Therefore, if the contracted daily attendance of 7½ hours is worked, the card will show both entries, AM and PM, against the same unit number above and below the card centre. For example, on Monday the start is shown as 08.00 hours, finishing at 16.30 hours, both entries being printed against Row No. 1. On Tuesday the start is in Row No. 3, finishing in Row No.5, representing a credit of two units, each of 15 minutes that is, half an hour. The differences, in positive or negative units, are entered each day in the appropriate box at the bottom of the card and at the end of each week they are totalled to establish the debit or credit balance for the week and this is entered in the appropriate credit or debit box at the top right corner of the card.

Advantages of a clock card system
 (i) Capital cost is low if only one clocking-in point is utilised.

Disadvantages of a clock card system
 (i) The psychological stigma and inherent resentment of 'clocking in'.
 (ii) When an employee is absent from his place of work there is no visual way of knowing whether the employee is at work or not.
(iii) The clock card may only show actual starting and finishing times, in which case the administration costs are increased due to the time spent in calculating actual hours and minutes worked.

The administration incurred with the line difference type recording scheme may be less than with other manual methods. However, some companies will be sceptical about using the line difference scheme in view of its approximation of actual hours worked.

Meter Recording

This is the most popular system of recording for fwh as it provides an objective record and is more readily acceptable to employees than conventional time clocks.
 The equipment consists of a master clock which is connected to

individual counters. These counters, in appearance and function, are not unlike a car mileometer. Each employee is allocated a counter which, when activated by his own personal key, records total attendance hours. The difference between this type of equipment and a conventional time clock is that it does not record actual starting and finishing times but simply the cumulative number of hours worked since the beginning of the settlement period. Time is metered in hours and hundredths of an hour and the master clock can be programmed to switch on and off at the beginning and end of a bandwidth within the 24 hour cycle, so that the time spent on site by an employee outside the bandwidth is not recorded. It can also be programmed to switch on and off at lunchtime if this is desired.

The equipment is usually installed in individual departments and/ or near to the employees' place of work, thus eliminating the queuing normally associated with 'clocking in'.

Illustrations of this type of equipment as supplied by two manufacturers are shown in Fig. 4.6 (Hengstler Flextime) and Fig. 4.7 (Haslertime).

Hengstler Flextime
The equipment consists of a master clock and slave units of recording counters which are available in units of eight or sixteen. These units (stations) can be located apart from each other but are all linked to a master clock. Each station incorporates the key accepting units and each counter is fitted with a push button reset which returns the counters to zero. The counters are covered by a lockable Perspex door.

The key acceptor is activated by a coded plastic key which is inserted into the slot by the employee on his arrival in the morning and whilst the key remains there his hours are metered on the counter and his presence is indicated by a red indication lamp.

The individual plastic keys provide a space for a photograph so that they can serve a dual purpose as a security pass.

A typical installation is shown diagramatically in Figure 4.8.

Haslertime
This equipment consists of a master time control unit and a series of personal time recording counters — one for each employee. There are ten personal recording counters in each recorder unit, but they can also be supplied in banks of five or twenty. Each employee operates the recording unit with his own personal key.

Fig 4.6 : METER RECORDING A Hengstler Flextime Station

Reproduced by kind permission of Hengstler Flextime Ltd.

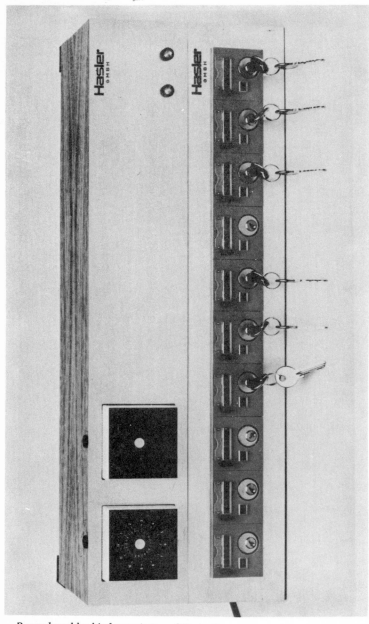

Fig 4.7 : METER RECORDING Haslertime Recorder Unit

When arriving at work, he simply switches on his recorder by inserting the key and turning it. The key is removed until he finishes work when he re-inserts it to switch the counter off. As the days pass, the number of hours worked are added up on the counter and continuously displayed. A green indicator shows whenever the unit is switched on, providing a simple way to see who is at work at all times. Each counter can be re-set to zero by using a meter key and depressing a push button, sited alongside the counter.

The recorder units are controlled by a master time control unit, consisting of a master clock and an optional clock for fixed breaks. This unit can be installed with a recorder unit (as shown in Figure 4.7) or can be installed at some remote point from which it can control a number of recorder units.

The reader will already have identified distinct similarities between the two systems, but there are enough significant differences in detail, (for example, cost and the degree of decentralisation possible) to pose a choice for the user.

Problems associated with meter equipment

(i) Meters record time in hours and hundredths-of-an-hour. This is a decimal system with which most people are unfamiliar and this can give rise to confusion and misunderstandings. This can be overcome by making a conversion table available at each station (or in some other convenient place). An example of such a table is shown in Fig. 4.9.

(ii) An employee may misplace his key or leave it behind at home. Spare sets of keys are provided by the makers of the equipment, and are normally held by the departmental manager. Master keys, which fit all meters, are provided for use in emergencies.

(iii) Employees may forget to activate or de-activate their meters each time they start or finish work. Where this does occur, it is normally found to be a transient phenomenon during the introductory period, but where it persists, the following methods of overcoming the problem have proved useful:

(a) making supervisors accountable for their employees' responsible use of the keys.

(b) displaying appropriate notices at exits.

(c) ensuring that management and supervisors use the equipment responsibly thus setting a good example.

61

Fig 4.8 : Hengstler Flextime Units — A Typical Installation

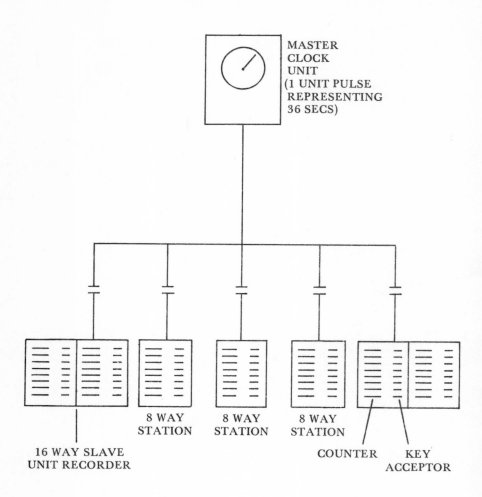

MASTER
CLOCK
UNIT
(1 UNIT PULSE
REPRESENTING
36 SECS)

16 WAY SLAVE
UNIT RECORDER

8 WAY
STATION

8 WAY
STATION

8 WAY
STATION

COUNTER   KEY
ACCEPTOR

Fig 4.9 : Conversion Table

Minutes as 1/100ths of an Hour					
Minutes	1/100	Minutes	1/100	Minutes	1/100
1	02	21	35	41	68
2	03	22	37	42	70
3	05	23	38	43	72
4	07	24	40	44	73
5	08	25	42	45	75
6	10	26	43	46	77
7	12	27	45	47	78
8	13	28	47	48	80
9	15	29	48	49	82
10	17	30	50	50	83
11	18	31	52	51	85
12	20	32	53	52	87
13	22	33	55	53	88
14	23	34	57	54	90
15	25	35	58	55	92
16	27	36	60	56	93
17	28	37	62	57	95
18	30	38	63	58	97
19	32	39	65	59	98
20	33	40	67	60	100

(d)   ensuring that employees leaving their keys in overnight or leaving their meter running by mistake are reprimanded the following morning and that an appropriate entry is made on their diary sheet. Some firms have adopted the policy of penalising an employee on each occasion that he leaves his key in the meter by debiting him with up to half an hour. However, one would be well advised to use this sanction sparingly during the period of introduction.

(iv)   The recording of short absences away from the work place may be required. In this respect most companies using meter equipment insist that an employee withdraws his key or switches off his meter when he leaves the site of his place of work. The reasons for this are:

(a)   To identify whether or not the employee is at his work place
(b)   As a control on employee absences.
(c)   In the case of fire, a Fire Evacuation Officer can immediately establish which employees were out of the building at the time of the fire alarm.

The recording of short absences away from a work place is a particular problem for those employees who are required by nature of their work to spend a considerable amount of time away from their organisation. This is particularly tiresome for senior staff who will find that approved absences of this nature will have to be recorded separately on a diary sheet.

However, Hengstler Flextime will supply an extra set of keys with their equipment, the keys being moulded in a different colour so that one can be issued to those employees involved in regular movement away from the organisation. The different coloured key can then be substituted for his normal key by the employee as he leaves the site and vice versa on his return.

The different coloured key then signifies that the employee is working, but not on the site. This facility is particularly useful to organisations with several separate sites in one town or city which necessitate considerable employee movement between them.

Advantages of a meter system
- (i)   A visual reading of hours recorded is always shown and is immediately available to an employee and his employer.
- (ii)   An indicator shows an individual's presence at work; a positive aid to supervisors.
- (iii)   It is a system of time recording which is not associated with the conventional time clock and, to the average employee, is more acceptable than 'clocking in'.
- (iv)   An employee is at his place of work before starting to record time. No longer can an employee 'clock in', often some distance from his work place, and then go to his locker room to change before he starts work. By the time he actuates his meter he should be ready to commence work.
- (v)   The long queues associated with conventional clock systems at finishing times are eliminated. This reduces employee frustration and has an indirect effect on production, in that employees no longer finish up to ten minutes early to 'get in the queue'.
- (vi)   Each individual holds his own key. There can be no duplicity or fraud since only the employee can activate his personal meter.
- (vii)   The concept of punctuality is eliminated, since no absolute starting time or finishing time is recorded.
- (viii)   The key can be modified to act as a company pass badge. Security is thus improved and/or simplified.

Disadvantages of a meter system
- (i)   Although a visual reading of hours accrued is always shown, inevitably there will be occasions when an employee is absent from his place of work (for example, through sickness or company business) and this absence will need to be recorded separately.
- (ii)   An employee may from time to time forget to record time or may leave his key in the meter by mistake, despite the fact that this is under close supervision.

Other manufacturers of meter systems
It would obviously be impossible to describe the complete range of meter equipment now being marketed in the UK by various manufacturers. This is obviously an expanding market and a list of current suppliers of all types of equipment known to the authors is given on page 176.

Reconciliation of contracted hours with hours worked, using a meter type system

It is necessary, at the end of each settlement period, to reconcile the actual hours recorded on the meter with the revised contracted hours.

Because the meter can only record actual hours worked at a particular work place, it is necessary, at the end of each settlement period, to carry out a process of adjustment and reconciliation. Adjustment is the process of subtracting from, or adding to, the contracted hours for the settlement period and, in order to do this, the following information is required.

Absences from work, whether paid or unpaid. (Sickness, holidays, etc.)	— usually recorded on diary sheet	*x hours*
Other absences on company business	—usually recorded on diary sheet	*y hours*
Other time, not recorded on the meter, but which is to count as attendance (for example, key not inserted).	— usually recorded on diary sheet	*z hours*
	Total	$(x + y + z)$ hours

From this total is subtracted:

Any time recorded by the meter, through the key being left in by mistake, when the individual is not present.	— usually recorded on diary sheet	*m hours*

This gives a Total Adjustment Hours of *$(x + y + z - m)$ hours,* and may be a positive or negative quantity. It is subtracted from the Contracted Hours to give the Revised Contracted Hours. Thus, Revised Contracted Hours = Contracted Hours minus Total Adjustment hours.

Reconciliation is the process of comparing the revised contracted hours against the actual meter hours recorded. To the balance produced are added/subtracted the credits/debits allowed in the rules and brought forward from the previous month to give a carry-over debit/credit to the following month.

Before proceeding to examine a typical diary sheet, it must be stressed that the terminology and method need not necessarily be the same in every organisation. What is important is that an adjustment be carried out to allow for (a) absences which, though not recorded by the meter, count as time attendance and (b) attendances which, through some discrepancy, have not been recorded on the meter.

The Diary Sheet
An example of one of the simplest forms of diary sheet is shown as Figure 4.10.

A diary sheet is issued to each employee at the beginning of a period with the following information completed:
Name
Personnel Number
Department
Four or five week period ending Friday
Contracted hours per settlement period

The employee records any absences, for whatever reason, on the right hand side of the form against the appropriate day. The information required is completed in the columns.'Hours/hundredths-of-an-hour' and 'Reason for absence', and the supervisor checks the entry and initials it. Debit records are also entered here for time recorded on the meter by mistake, for example when an employee leaves his key in over the lunch break. Of course, absences taken out of flexible working do not require an entry on the diary sheet. On the last day of the settlement period, the employee calculates the 'total adjustment hours', enters it below 'contracted hours', and subtracts it to arrive at the 'revised contracted hours'. From his meter he records the 'actual hours' and enters his 'credit/debit brought forward from last month' to calculate the 'current debit/credit to be carried forward to the next month'. The employee signs his sheet and passes it on to the supervisor for checking and approval before leaving work. In cases where the employee is absent from work on the last day of the settlement period, the supervisor should complete the diary sheet on behalf of the employee. It is necessary for the supervisor to check the entries, and in particular the meter reading on the last day of the settlement period as it is normal practice to re-set the meter to zero before the beginning of the next settlement period starting on the first working day of the following week.

Fig 4.10 : A Diary Sheet for use with Meter System.

DIARY SHEET			
	HRS. : ⁄₁₀₀ HR.	REASON	DEPT. HEAD INT.
NAME: J. SMITH	**WEEK 1** M ____ :		
	T ___2__ : 00	visit to auditors	GB.
PERSONNEL No: 264.	W ____ :		
	T ____ :		
DEPARTMENT: Accounts Dept	F ____ :		
	WEEK 2 M ____ :		
4 OR 5 WEEK PERIOD – 4 week / 24ᵗʰ February 1973. ENDING FRIDAY	T ___7__ : 50	1 Day holiday	G B.
	W ____ :		
	T ____ :		
	F ____ :		
~~CONTRACTED~~ STANDARD HOURS (4 × 37½) 150 : 00.	**WEEK 3** M ____ :		
	T ____ :		
TOTAL ADJUSTMENT HOURS 16 : 00	W ____ :		
	T −1 : 00	LEFT KEY IN METER OVER LUNCH period	GB.
~~CONTRACTED~~ REVISED STANDARD HOURS 134 : 00.	F ____ :		
	WEEK 4 M ____ :		
ACTUAL HOURS RECORDED ON METER 135 : 60.	T ____ ' :		
	W ___7__ : 50	SICKNESS.	G B.
	T ____ :		
CREDIT OR DEBIT BROUGHT FORWARD FROM LAST MONTH + 2 : 00.	F ____ :		
	WEEK 5 M ____ :		
CREDIT OR DEBIT TO BE CARRIED FORWARD TO NEXT MONTH + 3 : 60.	T ____ :		
	W ____ :		
	T ____ :		
EMPLOYEES SIGNATURE J. Smith	F ____ :		
DEPARTMENT HEAD SIGNATURE G. Best.	:	OTHER ADJUSTMENTS	
DATE 24 / 2 / 1973	16 : 00	TOTAL ADJUSTMENT HOURS	

The re-setting of the meters to zero can be the responsibility of each supervisor, but in most installations this job is done by a security guard or member of the personnel department, and it is recommended that at the time the meters are zeroed a master record is made of all meter readings so that there is a master check list to accommodate the occurrence where an individual has not recorded his meter reading.

The scheme outlined above preferably requires an auditing procedure on an ad-hoc basis, probably carried out by a member of the personnel department or the person made responsible for the system. Auditing is necessary to ensure that there is compatibility in the interpretation of the scheme between individual departments.

Centralisation of calculations
In cases where an organisation decides that calculations are to be done centrally the following points must be considered.
 (i) There must be feedback to the employee who needs to know how he stands at the end of each week.
 (ii) There must be a record of full and part day absences.
(iii) Each employee's meter will need to be read at the end of each week in order to facilitate (i) above. One typical application is outlined below.

In each department, alongside the meters is posted a weekly "Departmental absence from site" form, see Figure 4.11,where the employee or his supervisor makes an entry recording an employee's absence for whatever reason. In cases where an employee makes an entry, this must be approved by the supervisor.

In the example, on the 13th March, D.Grantham was on holiday and he is credited with eight hours against his absence. Note that there is a pay instruction column which, in this case, indicates that this is a 'holiday-time allowed paid'. For details of these codes see page 52).

On the other hand, R.Webster, who left his key in his meter, after leaving work at 5 pm, is debited with one hour. Since this only involves adjustment at the reconciliation stage, no action is taken as in the pay column.

At the end of the week, a Flextime record sheet *(See Fig. 4.12)* is also posted on the noticeboard on to which each employee enters his weekly meter reading (col.a.). During the weekend shutdown period, the meter reading is checked by the security guard and the meter is zeroed, always provided that the check is correct. In

Flexible Working Hours

Fig 4.11 : Departmental Absence from Site Sheet

DEPARTMENT: Warehouse.   WEEK ENDING: 16.3.1973

DATE	NAME	REASON FOR ABSENCE	FROM	TO	TOTAL TIME		APP'D BY	PAY INSTR.
					HRS.	1/100 Hr.		
8/3	S. Grantham	Holiday	8.00	5.00	8	00	a.T	Hol TAP
14/3	L. morrison	Sick leave	8.00	5.00	8	00	a.T	S.P
15/3	W. Gray	Dentist	9.30	10.30	1	00	a.T	T.A.P
15/3	L. webster	Left key in lock by mistake	5.00	6.00	-1	00	a.T	

* To be completed by Department Manager at week end.

AUTHORISED: A. Turnbull

70

Fig 4.12 : Flexible Working Record Sheet

NAME	METER READING (a)		TIME CREDIT OR (DEBIT) (b) THIS WEEK		THIS MONTH		WEEK No. (c)	WEEKS IN PERIOD (d)
	HOURS	$\frac{1}{100}$ HR.	HOURS	$\frac{1}{100}$ HR.	HOURS	$\frac{1}{100}$ HR.		
D. GRANTHAM	41	02	+ 1	02	+ 1	02	3	4
R. MORRISON	31	00	− 1	00	+ 3	00	3	4
P. PARKINSON	34	60	+ 2	60	+ 2	06	3	4
G. SALT	41	30	+ 1	30	+ 4	30	3	4
W. COLEY	40	40	+ 0	40	− 1	20	3	4
R. WEBSTER	38	60	− 1	40	+ 3	32	3	4
S. ABLE	40	00	−	−	−	−	3	4
B. WINTER	41	23	+ 1	23	+ 0	67	3	4

FLEXTIME RECORD SHEET — DEPARTMENT: Warehouse

4/5 WEEK PERIOD ENDING: 23.3.1973   WEEK ENDING: 16.3.1973

CHECKED D. Bell.

888/17

71

cases where the security guard identifies a discrepancy the meter is left until the employee returns to work when a check is made by the individual employee with the security guard.

Unless a discrepancy is found by the security guard he removes both the 'Flextime record sheet' and 'departmental absence from site 'sheet' and delivers these sheets to the central point for calculation. When the calculations (b-d) are completed, the original 'Flextime record sheet' is returned to the departmental supervisor duly completed. The 'Flextime record sheet' is pre-perforated and the supervisor tears off the individual strips and hands the appropriate one to the employee, therefore providing him with a weekly reconciliation statement of his position in terms of credit/debit hours for 'this week', 'this month', 'week number' and 'number of weeks in settlement period'.

There are many alternative paperwork schemes to choose from dependant on the information which is required for the organisation. Some schemes are designed to be part of the wages payment system, others being treated as completely separate functions.

Computer Based Systems

Data Collection Systems
Several manufacturers of computer equipment have been experimenting with input data terminals that can be used by individual employees. In this way, details of stock movements, production progress, job times, etc., can be fed to the computer directly, in a language it can accept.

This method eliminates the tedium of converting manually recorded information (pad or printed form and pencil) into data acceptable to the computer, using skilled machine operators. Provided that the computer has been suitably programmed, it will, on receipt of the data, update and issue action instructions for the various control systems in the factory (stock, production, payroll, etc.).

Adaptation to flexible working hour systems
Several manufacturers have, in recent years, introduced computerised attendance recording systems, operating on the basis described above. Basically, each employee has his own personalised plastic badge which he inserts into a badge reading terminal *(See*

Fig 4.13 : Operation 'clock out' with a 'Feedback OS436 Terminal'

Reproduced by kind permission of Feedback Data Ltd.

Fig. 4.13) which is essentially an input data station. These recording terminals are installed at strategic points in the factory or organisation and are connected to a central unit which prepares the data in either paper tape or magnetic tape in computer compatible form. By modifying the input data stations, it is possible for employees to record authorised absences, overtime, time allocations on different sites etc, and by modifying the computer programme, it is possible to produce a printout of cumulative time and attendance as required.

Feedback Data Ltd.

This company uses a modification of their well tried data input system, and have produced a terminal unit which meets the needs of attendance recording. A simplified diagram of the system is shown in Figure 4.14 and it will be seen that the terminal, in this case, includes a dial-type clock which can be synchronised to a central impulse source and can be independent of local mains supply. This particular terminal is fairly sophisticated and has facilities for manual data input through four, edgemounted, 10 position rotary switches, in addition to facilities for reading a plastic badge card. Simpler terminals (which will, of course, handle less data) are also available. Although only three attendance recording terminals are shown connected to the central unit, the company claims that in its basic system, this central unit will handle up to fifteen terminals and, since each terminal is capable of handling 200 employees, it seems likely that this basic arrangement would meet the needs of most companies in the UK. Where a larger number of employees have to be accommodated (for example in multiplant operations using a central computer), enhancements and extensions are possible. A typical printout, as provided by Feedback Data Ltd, is shown as Figure 4.15.

British Olivetti Ltd

There appears to be great similarities in the principle of operation of the Feedback system and the Olivetti system. That is to say, there is an input data station, a controlling unit and an output unit. The TI 201 terminals *(See Fig. 4.16)* are installed at strategic points throughout the work area, coupled to a central controller. Each employee is given a laminated plastic badge bearing his name, works number, photograph and other personal details. In addition the badge can carry a 'core time indicator' in the form of punched holes.

**Fig 4.14 : Computerised System Showing 3 Attendance Recording
Terminals connected to a Central Unit.**

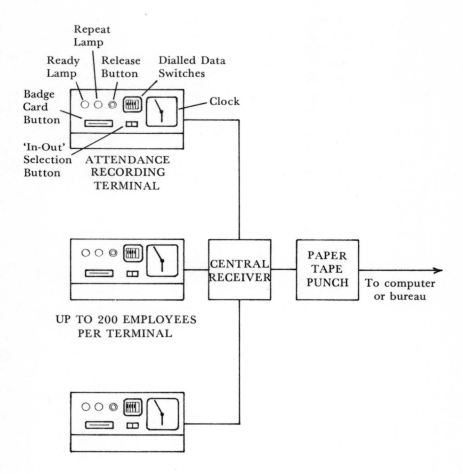

Reproduced by kind permission of Feedback Data Ltd.

75

Fig 4.15 : Example of Typical Computer Record of Hours Worked.
        (Supplied by Feedback Data Ltd.)

EMP NO	DEPT NO	DATE	MINUTES R	MINUTES F	MINUTES C	3RD PRN	TEA HOURS REC	TEA HOURS O/T	TEA HOURS C/T	REMARKS
		DATE 06/23/71				CUMULATIVE TIME AND ATTENDANCE REPORT				
1133	1CC1	C6/07/71								OUT
1133	1CC1	C6/C8/71						4.0		
1133	1CC1	06/C9/71					8.0			
1133	1CC1	C6/1C/71	1	1			8.0	3.7		
1133	1CC1	C6/11/71					8.0			
			1	1			24.0	7.7		
1134	1CC1	C6/07/71		3			8.0	4.1		
1134	1CC1	C6/C8/71					8.0			
1134	1CC1	06/C9/71		5			8.0	3.2		NZB
1134	1CC1	C6/1C/71								
1134	1CC1	06/11/71					8.0			
				8			32.0	7.3		MIN
1135	1CC1	C6/C7/71		5			6.9	2.1		
1135	1CC1	C6/C8/71		2			8.0	.3		
1135	1CC1	06/C9/71					8.0			
1135	1CC1	C6/1C/71	5				8.0			
1135	1CC1	06/11/71					8.0			
1135	1CC1	C6/12/71						8.0		NZB
1135	1CC1	C6/13/71							8.0	NZB
			5	7			38.9	10.4	8.0	MIN
1136	1CC1	06/C7/71	2				8.0			
1136	1CC1	C6/C8/71					8.0			
1136	1CC1	06/C9/71					8.0			
1136	1CC1	C6/10/71					8.0			
1136	1CC1	C6/11/71					8.0			
			2				40.0			

Fig 4.16 : Example of Employee Recording Using 'Olivetti TI201 Terminal'

Reproduced by kind permission of British Olivetti Ltd.

When an employee starts and finishes work each day, he reports it by inserting his badge into a TI 201 terminal. Here it is momentarily trapped, read and released. The coded works numbers etc. are read by the terminal and this information is transmitted over cable to a central controlling unit and paper tape punch. Here data and time are added and the whole message punched on to paper tape. This tape is used to enter attendance information into a computer which may perform the following functions:

  (i) Calculates total employee hours.
 (ii) Checks and reports clocking time vs core time infringements.
(iii) Prints 'credit' and 'debit' hours for each employee.
(iv) Calculates pay.
 (v) Analyses work patterns
(iv) Reports daily absentees.

TI201 terminals are also available with push buttons which are used to report 'exceptions' (sickness, excused absence etc).

Complex systems involving individual core times may be implemented without increased administrative complexity. Computer programmes are able to analyse work data and provide information on work patterns.

Advantages of computerised systems
  (i) The identity badge recording system is more acceptable to employees than the conventional clock card.
 (ii) Security — each member holds his own badge.
(iii) It allows the associated clerical and payroll tasks to be completely computerised thus reducing the administrative needs.
(iv) Input terminals can be designed and computer programmes modified to cover all eventualities — interruptions during core time, absences, etc.
 (v) Some types of input equipment may be used to record other information. (For example stores issue notes, inspection record, etc) and costs are therefore reduced.

Disadvantages of computerised systems
  (i) Unless the system has a direct link to a computer the employee will probably only receive a weekly reconciliation of his hours.

(ii) In addition to the expenditure on buying the terminals there is the cost of computer time.

(iii) There is no visual check on the employee's attendance for supervision.

(iv) Inevitably, from time to time, an employee will forget to record time and as there is no visual check this information cannot be identified until the weekly reconciliation of hours is produced.

(v) Decentralisation of stations is expensive due to the high cost of terminals.

The Cost of Recording Equipment

Although it is possible to achieve a flexible working hours scheme by recording time manually, the cost of its administration may be considerably more in the long-term, than by using the more objective method of time recording with some form of recording equipment.

The costs of an installation obviously vary depending on the number of employees to be included in the scheme and also the amount of decentralisation that is required. The following table gives a comparison of typical costs:

Recording System	Cost/Employee/Year*
Conventional Time Clocks	£0-25
Individual Meter System	£2-50 — £4-00
Computer based system with Punched Card or Tape Data Recording	£0-80 — £2-50†

Table 4.1

* The cost per employee year is based on purchase price spread over a five year period. It does not include installation costs, stationery nor CPU running time in the case of computer based systems.

† The computer based system cost is shown as that producing information in computer acceptable form only. It does not include the cost of processing equipment or 'renting' computer time which is approximated at £1.20 per year/per person.

This buying of computer time is, of course, the major variable cost with a computer system. There is no directly comparable variable cost with a clock or meter system, but it should be borne in mind that whereas the computer will 'process' the data, some form of manual or machine processing has still to be carried out in the case of clock or meter systems.

Some explanation is probably necessary, regarding the spread of estimated costs in Table 4.1.

Clock   Costs are based upon (i) an average cost of clock equipment, and (ii) an allocation of 120 employees per clock.

The clock costs are thus of a stepped variable type in which a step is necessary every time a separate clock is installed at a station, or a new station is opened. Thus costs could be disproportionately high if a large number of stations were needed to serve a relatively small number of employees based at a number of different locations.

Meter and Computer These systems have two separate stepped variable costs. The first is associated with the cost of the master unit (in the case of computers this is the Receiver, and in the case of meters, this is the Master Clock). These 'masters' can serve a certain number of slave units, and, as in the case of clock systems, (described above) they have a stepped variable aspect which operates every time a new station is inserted. The number of stations will obviously affect the total costs. *(See Fig. 4.18)*.

It is thus impossible to be specific about the cost of time-recording equipment until the whole question of employee numbers and location has been investigated and it is again emphasised that the figures in Table 4.1 must be interpreted in relation to typical installations.

For example, the figure of £2-50 for meters is based on a single master-nine station system serving seventy two people. This is the limit for a master with one particular manufacturer, and, if

80

Fig 4.18 : Effect of Number of Stations on Total Costs

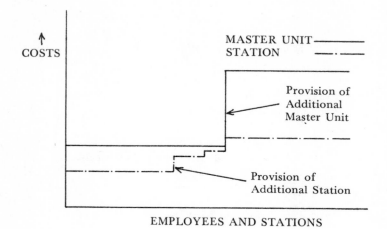

MASTER UNIT————
STATION   —.—

↑
COSTS

Provision of
Additional
Master Unit

Provision of
Additional Station

EMPLOYEES AND STATIONS

100 people were in the scheme, costs would rise. The same arguments would apply in computer systems and, of course, other meter systems.

It is absolutely necessary that, during the design stage *(See Chapter 6),* this whole aspect be investigated by the project leader and the steering committee if this exists.

However, cost is unlikely to be the only factor which the user will be concerned with in deciding which system of time recording to use. For example, computer systems are bound to be attractive to the user who is already operating a complete attendance/payroll system using either 'form and pencil' input or 'computer' input. Similarly, where time clock systems are already installed and the employees are conditioned to their use, modification and retention of this system would have its attractions. The whole question of choice is investigated further in Chapter 6 'Design and Installation'.

Summary

Four basic methods of recording are available.

(i) *The 'trust' system.* Each individual is responsible for writing down his various starting and finishing times, and any other data required (for example, absences from site, sickness, holidays etc.). At the end of the accounting period the information is collected and collated. This is done by the employee and/or a functional department.

   The system has the appearance of cheapness, but there are often hidden costs. It is not objective, yet may appear attractive to certain occupational groups.

(ii) *'Clock cards'.* A simple mechanical version of the 'trust' system. More objective but still requires computation and collation. Has operational disadvantages associated with queuing and psychological disadvantages with all work forces, but particularly with white collar workers. Capital costs are low but administrative costs are high.

(iii) *'Meters'.* Employees find this system very acceptable. Highly personalised and gives an immediate statement, at any point in time, of accumulated hours of attendance per settlement period. Still requires reconciliation of adjusted hours before a 'final statement' can be produced at the end of the month, and this can be done by employees and/or a functional department. Completely de-emphasises actual 'starting' and 'finishing times. Gives a visual indication of whether an employee is 'out' or 'in'. Capital costs higher than with previous two systems.

(iv) *'Computers'.* By feeding attendance information to a computer which has been suitably programmed, it is possible to operate a recording and computational system to control flexible working hours. A variety of input methods is available, but the most attractive use employee-operated input stations. Capital cost of these types can be high, but the main attraction is the possibility of integrating the flexible working recording/computing with a complete accounting and payroll system. Can provide printouts at any point in time, but if these are required frequently, running cost escalates. Must be linked to a computer or computer bureau, thus will be attractive to organisations already using computer time. Its major disadvantage compared with meter systems is its inability to give 'spot check' information (is an employee 'in' or 'out'? How many attendance hours has an employee accrued? etc).

5. Special Problems

It is now necessary to consider the special problems associated with specific situations and certain occupational groups when flexible working hours are introduced. The general problems associated with the design and introduction of a scheme are dealt with in Chapter 6, but it is necessary to identify, at this stage, where particular difficulties may arise.

Problems associated with Communications and Servicing

Customer Relations: In order to maintain effective customer relations the following aspects will need considering —

(i) *Opening Hours*
Under normal circumstances flexible working gives a wider bandwidth and it is highly probable that some employees will be at their work place outside the limits of what was previously the normal working day. This gives the organisation the opportunity to increase its opening hours to the public provided that:
(a) there are observed benefits in increasing opening hours
(b) a system of employee cover is devised to guarantee the extended hours of opening. In other words, this cannot be left to chance.

It is, of course, appreciated that this factor may not apply to many organisations in which there exists no direct, face-to-face contact with the public and/or customers. On the other hand, the question of opening hours could be important in local and national government offices and in the retail trade.

(ii) *Telephone and telex communications*
The hours during which an organisation can be contacted by telephone and telex are likely to be altered by the nature of changes in the spread of employee's hours within the various departments. The evidence is that the 'spread', or

84

bandwidth, of a department's operational time tends to increase, but organisations will be concerned to ensure that outside customers and suppliers can always contact a given department within a specified bandwidth.

Depending upon whether adequate cover can be arranged at the switchboard (see below) then a decision must be made as to whether it is desirable to *extend* the hours during which the organisation (and its departments) can be contacted by telephone and telex, or whether those hours should be *reduced*.

(iii)   *Notification of change-over*
Whatever decision is taken in (i) and (ii) above, a further decision is necessary as to the advisability of notifying all outside contacts of the changes envisaged. Though we are not aware of any organisations advertising an increased availability, some organisations are advertising their core time on their business notepaper; that is, a reduced availability. The significance of this notification may not be clear to customers, many of whom will see it as suggesting that they can only contact the organisation during the core period. In our view the publication of core time can be confusing to external contacts of the company, unless it is qualified by other information. There is no doubt that, in certain situations, such a publication may cause deterioration in customer relations.

Relations Within and Between Departments: In order to maintain effective vertical and horizontal relations within the organisation, the following aspects will have to be considered.

(i)   *Communications*
Here the arguments which held in customer relations (above) would be equally applicable within the organisation. Lateral communications can only be maintained if the availability of the personnel in each department is precisely defined. A similar argument would apply in the case of vertical communication between managers in the hierarchy. What is abundantly clear is that, as far as internal meetings are concerned then, unless adequate notice is given, they will have to be held in core time.

(ii)   *Servicing*
Here we are referring to that form of inter-departmental servicing without which functional departments in the organisation cannot operate. For example, if a production department cannot commence work unless an electrician and mechanic are standing by, and these craftsmen are located in a works engineers department, then, unless some dovetailing of start times and finish times takes place between the departments (or between individuals in the department,) production might suffer.

(iii)   *Departmental cover during the bandwidth*
One problem, which tends to span both inter and intra-departmental aspects, is whether there should be complete departmental cover throughout the bandwidth. The temptation to introduce this rule automatically is a strong one, but this decision should not be made until the pros and cons have been fully considered. It may be neither necessary nor desirable.

Generally speaking it has been found that, in practice, employees who are given the opportunity to work flexible hours are the first to recognise the need for limitations and will make their own restrictions without strong influence from management.

Problems associated with the Administrative Function

(i)   *Manning of a reception desk and telephone switchboard*
The nature of this function obviously imposes constraints on the amount of flexibility in working hours which can be offered to telephonists and receptionists. At the same time, decisions regarding opening hours and departmental availability (see discussion above) will obviously modify these constraints between organisations. For example, the organisation may decide that full cover of the new bandwidth is unnecessary.

Where, however, an increased bandwidth has to be covered, it may be possible to do this by staggering the hours of two or more persons performing the same jobs. However, a much more satisfactory method of tackling this aspect is to make the position quite clear to the employees concerned and emphasise that full cover is required and to put the onus on them to arrange their own flexibility provided that this is done.

(ii)   *Postal services*
The receipt (including opening) and dispatch (including signing) of correspondence via postal services may be disrupted unless suitable arrangements are made. This could involve special facilities for post opening at the start of bandwidth and/or a special postal collection at the end of bandwidth.

(iii) *Cleaning*
Where cleaning, in offices, has been done outside normal working hours, this may no longer be feasible. However, it may be possible to re-arrange cleaners' work programmes so that overlap at the extremes of the working day is minimised.

(iv)   *First aid and casualty cover*
If first aid cover is considered a necessity throughout the bandwidth then an organisation will have to review its present practices. Where a full time nurse is employed then cover for her absence may be required. The problem could be more complex in very large organisations, where a full medical and health service is offered to employees, or where statutory requirement exists. (*See section below on Legal Constraints*).

(v)   *Canteen (tea breaks and lunches)*
(a)   where teabreaks have been made optional and/or flexible, there is some evidence that employees tend to cut back on these .
(b)   flexible lunch breaks change the pattern of employees' arrivals.
(c)   lunch time usage may change, if there is flexibility in the lunch break.
Thus a careful record should be kept during the introductory period and management must be ready to accept that new types of services may be required.

(vi)   *Service functions*

These may have to be extended to cover the extremes of the bandwidth. For example, the heating system may have to be switched on, and the premises unlocked, at an earlier time than before.

Apart from routine security (locking up, fire dangers etc.), special consideration must be given to security in its widest sense, since there may be security risks associated with confidentiality when employees work alone, for fairly long periods, at the extremes of the bandwidth.

(vii) *External services*

Although it cannot be expected, nor is it necessarily desirable, to maintain a telephone switchboard throughout the total band width, it will be necessary to ensure that all employees working at the extreme hours of the day do have access to a telephone in case of an emergency. Instructions on getting outside assistance in case of fire or accident must be a consideration when drawing up a set of rules.

Problems associated with the Production Function

The term 'production' can be misleading, but here we are concerned with activities at the point where value is added to a product or goods when work is done on it in a manufacturing or servicing process. It would apply equally to a car assembly line, to a ship-yard and to a Parks Department, wherever they are.

In effect, we are concerned with the problems which fwh can create in job, batch and flow production, both for the employees involved and for management controlling the operation. If the words 'shop floor', or 'shop floor employees' are used, they should be interpreted as widely as possible. In our interpretation, a chamber maid in a hotel and a painter on the Forth Bridge would equally rank as production workers.

(i)   *Overtime*

From the employees' point of view this aspect will need to be completely resolved before the scheme is likely to be acceptable to them. They must be reassured that flexible working is not going to reduce their take home pay through a reduction in overtime payments. (The various ways of dealing with overtime are discussed in Chapter 2). Management will need to be very clear of its intentions on this issue before discussing it with both employees and unions. On the one hand flexible working has been said to reduce an organisation's overtime bill and on the other there have been many statements to the effect that fwh does not interfere with the employees' pay packet. An evaluation is necessary, and this must be carried out in relation to the organisation's needs.

(ii) *Recording of overtime*

Where meters are used for time recording then it will be necessary to have some separate record of overtime worked in order that premium rates can be calculated. In the authors' opinion it is better for a separate record to be made of overtime worked and probably one of the best ways of doing this is by using the traditional time clocks where they exist, so that an accurate record of actual starting and finishing times is maintained. In this way the appropriate overtime rates can be calculated.

(iii) *Restrictions on flexibility*

The amount of flexibility which can be given to shop floor workers may be less than that which can be offered to office workers. This is explored in more detail below, but it is as well to identify this possible source of dissension. In a society in which there is a movement to reduce the differentials between white and blue collar workers, it would be unfortunate if the introduction of fwh were to aggravate this situation. On the other hand, if it is possible to arrange comparable bandwidths for both staff and shop floor, not only would some of the present communication problems disappear (such as currently occur between staff and shop floor in many of our factories) but the goodwill generated would be tremendous.

(iv) *Job production*

This type of 'one-off' production is likely to have the lowest level of immediate interdependability between employees and thus offers a high degree of choice for the workforce within the flexible bands. However, it is dangerous to

89

generalise when the label 'job production.' is taken to cover the individual craftsmen working alone and, say, the building of a ship involving many hundreds of men.

It is true, of course, that even in job production, we sometimes find batch production techniques being used, but it is necessary to look at the range of operations as a whole and, if the particular project (like the building of a bridge) is regarded as one single operation in which all work is concentrated until completion, a reasonable differentiation can be made between this type of production and the others described below.

A characteristic of this type of work is that the labour force is usually highly skilled (often multi-skilled) and very versatile. In consequence, it is found that responsible control is usually exercised by the individual or group and this, of course, is an ideal situation for a successful application of fwh.

(v)   *Batch production*
This type of production is probably the most dominant type in use in the very large British manufacturing engineering industry, but is, of course, found elsewhere (manufactured food, clothing, footwear etc). Undoubtedly, introduction of fwh schemes would cause problems for production control staff and supervisors. Yet the very existence of batches of components provides a buffer against non-availability of an employee for a short period in the flexible bands. One might well suggest that the problems to be solved would be similar in nature to those now being solved daily, in batch production factories, when employees are absent through lateness, sickness or other causes. There are relatively few reports regarding applications of fwh to batch production processes in the UK but there is ample evidence from West Germany that, provided there is careful pre-planning by supervisors and production control, the system can be a success. For example Deeson[1] reports on the experience of a British engineering company in Germany, Vicker-Zimmer AG who have successfully applied a system since 1969. He points out that the flexible bands are narrow (between 07.15 and 08.15 and 16.15 and 18.00) and emphasises that the key to the success of the scheme is that *production*

employees must agree with their supervisors as to when they come and go. Another report, by Hammond [2] quotes the success of the Losenhausen machine factory in West Germany where some 300 production workers have split up into 8—12 main groups, of which five or six must be there at any one time. Each group makes itself responsible for manning a certain number of machines and co-operates with other groups in ensuring that production is maintained.

It would be irresponsible to claim that problems in this area are easily overcome. At this stage there is a dearth of hard data on which to draw significant conclusions. Nevertheless, there is an in-built flexibility in batch production which suggests that, despite the additional problems fwh might pose for production planners, it should be possible to offer batch production workers some choice at the extremities of the bandwidth.

More needs to be known about the 'rest' periods of batches which Lockyer [3] has identified as typical of batch production. These are the time periods during which no work is being done upon a batch (or a unit within a batch) during production.

Research in this area is obviously needed and it is possible that this might reveal that fwh would have a very marginal effect on operational indices like work-in-progress, unit production time, batch size etc.

(vi)   *Flow production*
A flow line (for example — a car assembly line) is basically inflexible, and the production rate must be appreciably constant. There are no buffer stocks between the work stations on the line and the absence of one member of the team manning the line will completely disrupt output. This degree of employee inter-dependability may appear, at first sight, to invalidate the concept of fwh in such an application. This, however, is not so. One solution is the provision of a *springer-arbeiter,* an employee who is multi-skilled and can man a gap in the assembly line. We are already familiar with this individual in large assembly lines in this country where he performs a relief function for employees who wish to visit the toilets. Obviously this could impose a heavy cost on the company unless the situation was tightly controlled, and this, of course, would tend to

reduce the benefits of fwh schemes.

A more positive approach, particularly on small production lines, is to develop the concept of team working. The authors are aware of two such applications in the UK. At one of these installations (Riker Laboratories) women workers on packaging lines (having between 8 and 10 work stations) have accepted that they cannot have complete freedom of choice and the working times of the lines are agreed by each team rather than by individuals. The arrangement appears to work most successfully and, to date, there is no record of a line stopping production through causes which could be attributed to fwh.

(vii)   *New trends in production methods*
A discussion on applicability of fwh to production areas would not be complete without some mention of the experiment now being introduced to replace the repetitious, boring work of assembly line production with a system of team working. Phillips of Holland have, in fact, experimented for many years along these lines, but an 'innovation' in Sweden with Volvo/Saab car production is of more recent origin and its impact is likely to be more far-reaching. Here the workers have been organised into assembly teams and each team is responsible for the production of a sizeable sub-unit of production (sizeable in terms of work content and complexity). This re-thinking has been forced upon the Swedish car manufacturers by their labour force's increasing rejection of the whole concept of linear, balanced, flow production, in which the work content at each station is highly simplified. Saab's commitment to the new approach is demonstrated in the building of a new factory for car engines, in which bays have been constructed for the assembly teams, who will operate within a defined territory. (It is worth noting that Lotus Cars, Norwich, have used this system of production for many years, but this is the first example of a high volume mass production car firm abandoning Ford's classic concept, developed at Highland Park in 1914).

If approaches of this type become common, then there is no doubt that fwh would be more readily applicable to mass production techniques. It will be interesting to observe whether a demand for fwh lends weight to the other 'accelerators' (high absenteeism, low output, industrial strife etc), in influencing patterns of high-volume production methods over the next decade.

(viii) *An integrated experiment*

Possibly one of the most highly ambitious experiments encompassing both office workers and shop floor employees, is the report by Willatt[4] on Brown Boveri of Switzerland (BBC). This company introduced flexible working for its 16,000 employees and courageously decided that it should apply to all categories of staff and work. Willatt reports that a much longer period of adjustment was needed on the shop floor than among the office staff, and the problem appears to have been complicated by the wide variety of production methods used. Thus, some employees worked individually, some in groups, some on high precision engineering and others worked on assembly line production. (Some departments also operated a two-shift system).

(a) *Shiftworking*

BBC allows a flexible band, at the beginning of the day shift (between 04.51 hrs and 05.51 hrs) and a flexible band at the end of the afternoon shift (22.30 hrs and 23.09 hrs). The changeover time of the two shifts is fixed at 14.00 hrs and this is mandatory. Incidentally, BBC insists that supervisory staff must be present between 04.15 hrs and 23.09 hrs.

(b) *Group working*

BBC fabricates turbines and generators and in group job (or project) production of this type the departmental head is made responsible for ensuring that the variable-time arrangements made by the members of the groups dovetail in with overall production requirements.

(c) *Assembly line*

In the assembly of small electric motors by women, the supervisor is required to make himself responsible for a steady flow of components and assemblies despite the fluctuation in the level of workforce available during the flexible bands. This is done largely by a system of buffer stocks.

Thus, in one large manufacturing organisation, it does appear that, given a readiness by management to innovate, supervisors and workforce respond favourably. BBC confess that, before the introduction of the scheme, supervisors greatly feared the disruption and complication of schedules which would result. In the event, their fears were unfounded. If working patterns have changed, these have taken place, reports Willatt, uniformly rather than haphazardly, and work rhythm has been unaffected.

Problems Associated with Certain Occupational Groups

WHITE COLLAR EMPLOYEES GENERALLY

(i)   *Resistance to time recording*
       The most common problem encountered with staff and other white collar groups is resistance to the concept of time recording. This is dealt with elsewhere *(See Chapters 4 and 6)* and will not be elaborated here.

(ii)   *New attitudes to employer/employee relationships*
       The argument that emphasis on an attendance norm will alienate employees who see themselves as 'part of the firm' is a debatable proposition. The impact of mergers and bureaucratisation has effectively destroyed such special relationships as ever existed between white-collar workers and their employers and in the 'new' white collar fields (computers, data processing) has never been an important factor. Where it does arise, this problem is likely to occur among more senior, managerial staff.

MANAGERS

The position of managers, as a special category of the white collar group is now examined.

(i)   *Time recording*
       The argument against recording appears to be based on three premises —
       (a)   it lowers the status of managers in the eyes of their subordinates.

(b)   it implies some form of mistrust by their superiors.

(c)   since managers are generally task orientated, and not bound to contracted hours of attendance, time recording is unnecessary.

The first two arguments can be overcome by persuading the manager that status is an intangible and that his rating (in the eyes of his staff) may very well rise; and that his superiors, far from mistrusting him, depend upon him to set an example which will help overcome the resistance of his staff to time recording.

The third argument is conceded and some managers report tendencies towards 'clock-watching' when they become aware, sometimes for the first time, of the long hours they are working. On the other hand, there is often satisfaction that superiors, in an objective way, are also now informed of this fact. This leads, naturally, to the next problem.

(ii)   *Time off*

If managers are to be required to time record, are they also to be allowed the benefits of fwh schemes? There is, in fact, no logical reason why managers should not have credit-time off, provided that they comply with the requirement that the work of the organisation does not suffer in any way. Undoubtedly, the introduction of fwh will throw this whole question into relief and it will be interesting to observe the answers which it provides.

(iii)   *Allowances for absences on company business*

This is likely to be a contentious area with managers who spend a great deal of time travelling on company business. Many organisations have taken the view that, when absent for a complete day the allowance will be equivalent to a *normal* working day. This ignores the fact that travelling may involve the manager in excess hours on company business. One company operating fwh in the UK allows 3 hours for travelling where that travel exceeds 200 miles, but no allowance is made for less than 200. Each organisation must decide on allowances for this type of duty. The same problem will arise regarding time allowance for business lunches. There is an argument that the whole period should be regarded as work and credit given accordingly

95

or, alternately, that a 'minimum break' period should be deducted. The problem will vary, according to the nature of the lunch break (fixed or flexible) but organisations must consider this before writing their rules.

(iv)   *Manager and secretary situation*
It is possible to exaggerate this situation although, initially, managers may feel it necessary to limit their secretary's freedom of choice in working hours. The situation is best solved by goodwill on both sides and providing the manager is prepared to re-think his work relationship with his secretary, the problem is soon resolved. Some managers claim that they welcome the opportunity to work part of the day free from interruptions from their secretary.

SUPERVISORS

As the essential link between management and operatives, supervisors may perceive special problems.

(i)   *The recording system*
The responsible use of the time recording system by his work group must be monitored by the supervisor. No other manager is in a position to effectively carry out this task. Thus it is important that the rules make absolutely clear the authority of the supervisor to check all time recording and reconciliation.

(ii)   *Supervisory cover*
Supervisory cover at the extremes of the bandwidth is bound to be limited, unless the supervisors increase their own working hours, which would be undesirable. The problem can be overcome by:
(a)   the supervisor delegating minor levels of supervision at the extremes of the bandwidth and/or
(b)   the supervisor checking each evening on the following day's workload for a particular employee, before deciding whether that employee can start work, on the following day, without supervision.

(iii)   *Team work*
Team, or group work, poses particular problems *(See*

Production Problems above). The supervisor may have to insist that time recording can start when all members of the team are present, except in cases where preparatory work can be done by one or two members of the group.

(iv)   *Rule observance*
The supervisor will always have to assume the role of 'referee-on-the-spot' in ensuring that the rules of the scheme are observed. The onus is upon him to make sure that he is completely confident in his handling of queries and interpretations. It is equally the responsibility of senior management to ensure that their supervisors interpret the rules in such a way that parity exists between all work groups. This can only be done by rigorously briefing and training the supervisors in interpretations.

Problems Associated with Legal Constraints

Statute Law
Statutory requirements may impose constraints on certain aspects of fwh schemes. The two Acts which are likely to concern most employers in the UK are the Factories Act of 1961 and the Offices, Shops and Railway Premises Act 1963. Apart from the following reference, neither of these Acts contains references to hours of work or to meal or rest breaks.

Section 175 of the Factories Act 1961 stipulates that, as regards women and young persons

(i)   *Total hours*
(a)   the total hours worked per day (exclusive of time allowed for meals and rest) must not exceed nine.
(b)   the total hours worked per week (exclusive of time allowed for meals and rest) must not exceed forty-eight.

(ii)   *Span of hours*
A daily period of employment must not exceed eleven hours, and must not commence before seven o'clock in the morning nor end later than eight o'clock in the

97

evening. (For young persons under the age of sixteen, the working day must not end after six o'clock in the evening, but with the raising of the school leaving age this year (1973) this should present no problem.)

(iii)   *Meals and rest breaks*
    (a)   a continuous spell of work must not exceed four and a half hours without a meal break of at least half an hour.
    (b)   a continuous spell of work may continue for five hours before the half hour break is taken, provided that a ten minute break is allowed during the five hour period.
    (c)   no one may be employed during a meal or rest break.

(iv)   *Uniformity of employment hours*
Employment and rest periods (as defined in accordance with (i), (ii) and (iii) above) will be uniform for all women and young persons within a given factory (except that young persons under sixteen may finish earlier. See (ii) above).

The observance of these requirements will obviously have to be borne in mind when designing a fwh scheme *(see Chapter 6)* but it must be immediately obvious that this section of the Act poses many problems.

What appears to be central to these problems is whether the existence of a given bandwidth, within which women and young persons exercise choice regarding starting and finishing times and overall length of the working day, constitutes a breach of (iv) above. To the knowledge of the authors, this has not been challenged by HM Factory Inspectorate, but it is a possibility which cannot be excluded.

(v)   *Other Statute Law*
In addition to the two main Acts mentioned above, employers would do well to examine the various Regulations and Orders for Safety, Health and Welfare in Miscellaneous Industries and, where a regulation or order applies to their organisation, ensure that the inception of a fwh scheme does not cause it to be unwittingly breached. For example, the Chemical Works Regulations, 1922,

stipulates in para 13 that a responsible person should always be readily available *during working hours* (authors' italics) whose duty it is to summon an ambulance in case of accident or sickness.

It appears that what would need to be established in a chemical works is what, under the fwh scheme, now constitutes *working hours* and if, as is more than likely, it encompasses the whole bandwidth, how the additional cover can be provided (See 'First Aid and Casualty Cover' in Administrative Problems above).

Common Law

In addition to possible liability under statute law, employers must also be aware of their responsibilities under common law and, in particular, how the introduction of a fwh scheme affects that responsibility.

The duty of an employer to 'take reasonable care' for the safety of his workmen is paramount and all other rules and principles are subject to this principle. The duty of taking reasonable care has been variously defined, but that by Lord Herschell (in Smith v Baker 1895 AC 325 HL)

"so to carry on operations as not to subject those employed by the employer to unnecessary risks",

seems to be generally acceptable.

The lesson here is clear. Where a system of fwh is likely to change the way in which 'operations are carried on', employers must consider the additional risks generated. For example, at the extremes of the bandwidth it may be necessary to stipulate that individuals do not work alone, in certain hazardous situations. The definition of hazardous is not easy and employers may prefer to play safe by imposing a blanket requirement that individuals cannot start work on their own.

The problem may be put in another way, if we consider the question of altered supervision patterns after the introduction of fwh. The duty of care has been defined by Lord Wright (Wilsons and Clyde Coal Co v English (1938) AC 57) as "a threefold obligation, the provision of a competent staff of men, adequate material and a *proper system and effective supervision*". (authors' italics).

It has been suggested above (Supervisors Problems) that the question of supervisory cover over the bandwidth might be solved in a number of ways. But the operational solution may involve the employer in additional risk at common law. Exactly how much emphasis should be given to this is a question for the employer to answer. But whatever that answer, it is bound to affect his final decision regarding supervision under fwh.

These two examples should indicate the importance of common law liability. Together with the more specific requirements of statute law, this must be recognised as a problem area, of varying importance, for many organisations.

(1)   Deeson, A.F.L. *Works Management* No 25 July/August 1972 p.4.
(2)   Hammond, B *Business Administration* Jan 1972 p.17
(3)   Lockyer, KG *Factory Management* — 2nd Edition Pitman London 1969
(4)   Willat, M *Financial Times Article* 29/12/72

6. The Design and Installation of a Scheme

General Introduction

When an organisation decides that the time is right to introduce a system of fwh the inevitable question must be faced; "how are we to go about it?"

The answer to this question will obviously depend upon the type and size of the organisation. Some will endeavour to introduce a complete scheme across the board. Others may decide that it is necessary to restrict the initial experiment to some areas or a few departments. Some will feel that it can be applied in manufacturing industry as well as in offices, whereas there will be others who will argue that it is nigh impossible to introduce it on the shop floor. In the authors' view, management who discount it for their shop floor employees may be doing themselves a great disservice, since the additional problems that a manufacturing function creates are often outweighed by the tremendous spirit of goodwill that can be obtained from the shop floor employees through its introduction. In many ways, the advantages offered to the shop floor outweigh those offered to staff. For instance, there are many office employees who already have the privilege of "nipping out" from their place of work to conduct private business, or for that "overdue hair cut", whereas the shop floor operators have never experienced these "perks" and often respond well to the extra freedoms which fwh gives. There are obviously many situations where fwh has yet to be applied, but experience in Europe has led to trials in shift working and in areas which previously were completely discounted. One of the greatest problems occurs on a four shift conveyor line situation and, whilst it might prove extremely difficult to apply fwh here, there are always a number of service and support functions whose staff could well be given an opportunity to participate in such a scheme. (For a discussion on fwh in production areas see Chapter 5.)

Timing

It is not intended to spell out the need for management to ensure that its "timing" of the introduction of a scheme of fwh is right. On the other hand, the importance of timing must not be overlooked and should be carefully considered at the inception. To attempt an introduction in the middle of a spell of bad industrial relations, for example, might be unwise. Each situation will need to be looked at carefully.

Commitment by Top Management

As with any organisational innovation, there is obviously a need for a commitment by top management to see that it succeeds. Without such support it is very unlikely to do so. Top management will find that they will need to be involved in at least some of the discussions and in the major part of the decision making, and this is possible only if they are fully committed, and understand the full implications of the scheme. Before a feasibility study on fwh is conducted within an organisation they will need to ask themselves "What are we hoping to achieve from it?" On the one hand, some employers will simply see it as an improvement to existing employee benefits whilst others will expect certain benefits to accrue for management, for example a reduction in labour turnover. Whatever the motive, other alternatives to the perceived benefits should be explored and assessed before a final commitment is made. Having made such a decision, it should then be made clear to everyone in the organisation that it has the blessing and full hearted support of senior management.

The Project Leader

Whatever the size of the organisation, whether it be large or small, it is advisable to appoint a project leader to co-ordinate the activities required in introducing a scheme of fwh. The time base element of a project of this nature will depend upon the size and complexity of the installation, but experience so far suggests that it must be well planned and that an application may take three months for between 500 and 1000 employees. The person appointed to the task will have to be able to talk to all levels of staff, including top management and shop floor, and should be someone who has experience in managing people and implementing projects of this nature. The type of person who could handle such a project is likely to be found among personnel officers, p.a.'s to senior management, Work Study or O & M specialists. On the other hand, some very large organisations may have project managers available, whose activities incorporate the field of personnel work.

Whoever is selected, he will need to have the full confidence and support of top management. He should report to a senior manager or director to whom he can refer for decisions, as he will inevitably find himself in a position of conflict from time to time.

Steering Committees

In organisations where there is union involvement or a works council and possibly in other non-union organisations, careful consideration should be given to the assistance which may be provided to the project leader by the setting up of a steering committee consisting of representatives of management and employees. This may prove a useful aid to organisations where an initially unfavourable employee reaction is a possibility. However, with the passage of time and as fwh becomes a more familiar concept to both management and workers in this country, then the need for a steering committee role may be reduced although it can be argued that there will always be a place for such a committee in this type of situation. It will also prove a useful sounding board or clearing house for the project leader.

The Tasks facing the Project Leader and the Steering Committee

(i) *Background Knowledge and Information*
As time goes by and more information becomes available on fwh schemes which have been introduced and their subsequent effect on organisations, the role of the project leader and the steering committee will become easier. However, their first task will be to research all past knowledge and experience before reaching any conclusions on the type of scheme which will best suit their particular circumstance.

Mention should be made of the assistance which is offered by the manufacturers of time recording equipment in Britain. Obviously, these companies tend to bias their advice in favour of their own equipment but, provided this is allowed for, they can offer valuable help regarding general aspects of fwh schemes as well as about time recording equipment in particular. (A list of current suppliers known to the authors is shown in

Appendix III.) At the same time, copies of the rules which are now being used by companies successfully operating fwh schemes should be sought. Many of these organisations are prepared to give information about such rules and may also release details of the findings of attitude and other surveys conducted both pre- and post-installation. The names of these forerunners are often quoted and many articles have appeared in the press and journals during the past year or so. Another source of information which may be useful is through the University and Polytechnic Libraries, for there is an increasing number of theses and reports which are being written on the subject by students, and many of these carry extensive surveys on both continental and UK experiments. Help may also be sought from the professional bodies and societies including the Industrial Society, British Institute of Management and Institute of Personnel Management. Of course, it is hoped that this book will provide the reader with most of the information that he requires and thus reduce the need to carry out extensive individual research.

Another useful approach is for the project leader to arrange to visit an organisation or company operating fwh. This can be of particular interest where the industry and function are similar and first hand experience can be directly related. However, one word of warning: it is dangerous to copy another scheme without considering its likely effect within one's own organisation (see Chapter 6), for there will rarely be two identical situations and transplants are often singularly unsuccessful. On the other hand, providing refinements are made and, to continue our gardening analogy, the ground well prepared, it is sometimes possible to copy a ready made scheme to advantage.

(ii) *Union Reaction*

As far as can be ascertained only a handful of unions have given their full support to the principle of fwh and there has been little union involvement to date.

In some applications the unions have taken an equivocal position and, while officially disapproving of fwh schemes have been prepared to 'sit on the fence' providing the employees of the organisation were in agreement to the trial. It is possible that with the passage of time their attitudes will become more positive and their involvement much greater. It is difficult to see how they can maintain a negative attitude in view of the generally positive response of employees participating in schemes so far.

Whatever the outcome, there are obvious aspects of the subject on which trade unions will want assurances, such as treatment of overtime, and this and their attitude towards it are discussed in detail in Chapter 9.

Thus a major task facing the project leader and his steering committee in a unionised organisation is to involve the unions at an early stage and, if it is not possible to obtain their wholehearted support for the scheme, attempt to obtain assurances that they will not sabotage the innovation. As suggested above, this task will be made the easier if unions are represented on the steering committee.

(iii) *Time Recording Systems*

Details of different types of recording systems which are known to the authors are detailed in Chapter 4. However, there are many organisations which are working fwh without any special equipment at all. These tend to be the relatively small and often informal organisations where the need for a system of recording is considered both unnecessary and undesirable. There are others who have continued to use their existing system (whether it is manual or mechanical), and this approach, if it is possible, has many advantages, both on cost and employee-acceptability grounds. The number of companies that have adapted conventional time clock recording for use with fwh is not known, but it is probably quite high in comparison to those who have installed special devices. A decision on the most suitable type of recording equipment to use within an organisation should be made after consideration of the following factors.

(a) *Work technology*
   The work technology of an organisation imposes a social and work structure which tends to be unique to that production or service function. Compare, for example, the socio-technical structure in a foundry and an insurance office.

(b) *Type of employee*
   Manual workers, technical or office staff.

(c) *Recording system used before fwh*
   Type of recording system will depend upon that used in the organisation prior to fwh. For example, an organisation that has not expected its staff to 'clock-in', in the past, may prefer

105

to use a meter or computerised system in preference to a conventional time clock, due to the resistance which would inevitably arise from the employees, to the latter.

(d) *Size of organisation*
A small company of, say, 10 people could operate fwh without any form of time control, if this is considered desirable. At the other extreme a company of, say, 5000 employees would need to have a more objective record of hours worked by its employees.

(e) *Cost*
The cost of the different types of recording systems vary and there is also a difference in the price of the same type of equipment as supplied by competitors. A table of comparative costs is shown on page 79.

(f) *Availability of administrative staff for reconciliation of hours worked*
Some forms of recording, for example, the manual system, may be cheap in terms of capital outlay, but expensive in time spent in the reconciliation of hours worked. If staff are already available, and the work of reconciliation can be dovetailed into existing work, this might be a deciding factor.

(g) *Decentralisation of equipment*
Where decentralisation is preferred, and some form of objective time recording is desired, then the meter system, which can be sited in individual departments, is the most economical method. The clock card system does not lend itself to decentralisation for departments of less than, say, 20 persons.

(h) *Accuracy and objectivity required*
As discussed in Chapter 4 some forms of recording rely on the 'swings and roundabouts' effect, and this may not be acceptable to some organisations or to a workforce. Also by the inherent nature of individual frailty, a manual system cannot hope to give the same accuracy as that of an objective time recorder.

106

(i) *Use of terminals for purposes other than time recording*
Some of the computerised terminals can be used as a computer input for other information on machine job times, etc, as well as for time recording.

(j) *Supervision*
By their nature some forms of recording require extra control by supervisors. On the other hand some can provide an aid to supervisors in addition to extra chores. For instance, the meter system provides the supervisor with the additional job of checking the correct and proper use of equipment, but it has the significant advantage of providing him with an immediate check on an employee's presence at work. This often becomes a priority where a system of fwh is introduced in an organisation where employees arrive and depart at different times.

(k) *The time employees spend away from the building*
Recording of employee's time spent away from the building can present particular difficulties where objective time recording equipment is used, and whilst there is no perfect system so far, some types of equipment lend themselves to this better than others.

(l) *Recording of time worked outside a normal working day*
Some types of equipment are specifically designed to switch on and off at the beginning and end of the a.m. and p.m. flexible bands; for example, the meter system. Where employees are likely to work outside the normal bandwidth and are required to record these hours then, where a meter system is selected, an alternative method of recording irregular hours would need to be devised.

(m) *Recording of overtime*
When overtime is worked and a record of actual overtime start and finish times are required for calculating premium payments, it will be found that some equipment lends itself to this function more than others (for example, a conventional time-clock system). This aspect would have to be taken into account, together with consideration of a possible manual system to supplement mechanical/electrical equipment.

Main Principles of the Scheme

The project leader/steering committee will probably be required to make recommendations to senior management on the main principles of the scheme fairly soon after they have completed their research. The main principles that need to be resolved at this stage are:

(i) *Length, Scope and Size of Experiment*
The type of question which would need to be answered here is "who is to be included in the trial?" — "will it be the whole organisation or simply one or two departments?". In large organisations the decision might be made to start the trial in one or two areas so that its effect on operations could be measured before introducing the scheme throughout. On the other hand, small organisations will probably decide to introduce it to all of their employees from the outset. The length of the experiment will vary between organisations, but it is suggested that three months is probably the shortest period in which the results can be assessed. Some trials have run for up to a year.

In considering the scope and size of the experiment, decisions will be affected by the function of the organisation and the different tasks which it performs. Of the installations so far carried out, many have initiated trials in one or two departments extending the scheme as its effect on the organisation emerges. Others have preferred to introduce it uniformly throughout the organisation, and in general terms the latter appears to be the more acceptable method to the employees, although in a large multiple business this may be impracticable due to the many problems which size and complexity create. Thus the setting up of a large experiment requires a considerable involvement by the project leader/steering committee and company resources generally, and these may not necessarily be available. When a decision is made to limit the size and scope of a trial the selection of the sections or departments to be included will have to be considered. This will depend to some extent on the complexity of the functions, but it is suggested that it would be unwise to take those departments which are considered the easiest to which to apply a scheme of fwh, without giving some thought to the problems that will arise in other departments or sections and how they might be overcome. On the other hand it is unlikely that a project leader/steering committee would go to the opposite extreme and choose for the initial experiment, those

108

departments which would be most liable to create problems. A balance between the two extremes is the best solution. If a decision is taken to introduce fwh department by department, then it is recommended that a timetable is worked out in terms of the trial and implementation.

(ii)   *Bandwidth — Flexible and Core Times*

The amount of flexibility that an organisation can allow will obviously depend upon technology and function. For instance, it is unlikely that a company with batch production or conveyor lines would be in a position to allow as much flexibility as in, say, an R & D function, where the norm is to work non-rigid hours. In fact, in production situations it is likely that there will be more restrictions on flexibility than in offices. Whatever the function, given this constraint it is advisable that, in any initial experiment, the amount of flexibility should be modest, so that if the scheme is successful the flexible bands can be increased later. This theory also applies to debit/credit carry over to the next period and time off in core time. It should always be remembered that it is much simpler to extend the bandwidth and periods of flexibility after an experimental period than it is to narrow them. A rash decision, made at an early stage, may be regretted later when it is too late to retrieve the situation. Many of the organisations that, from the start of the trial, have made it clear to the participants that extensions to the flexible periods will be considered if the scheme proves successful have found that they have been able to meet this promise. This has given an additional spin-off because many employees have done their utmost during the trial period to ensure that the scheme works well, hoping to persuade management to extend the flexible bands later.

Whilst it may generally prove less acceptable to management to put production employees on a wide bandwidth, it may be that in so doing management may be imposing restrictions which are unnecessary. For instance one UK company has found that the production staff are not interested in stopping on later than their previously fixed finishing time, whilst in the same company's offices there has been a tendency for some employees to work much later in the evening. If such an experience is typical, a company could stipulate the same bandwidth for both white and blue collar workers in the knowledge that the latter will normally start and finish work earlier than the counterpart office staff.

109

From the experiments carried out so far, there is evidence that most employees quickly fall into a pattern of working hours. These may well be different from their previous finishing and starting times, but they are likely to remain fairly constant for the individual employee. Obviously there will be the exception, for example, where the employee does not hear the alarm clock, or he decides to have a hair cut on his way to work, making him start work later on that particular day, but in most instances individual employees normally vary their starting and finishing times within very small bands.

(iii) *Size of Credit and Debit Carry-over to Next Settlement Period*

(iv) *Time Allowed off in Core Time (Half or Whole Day Absences)*

(v) *Treatment of Overtime*

(vi) *Time Allowances for Medical and other Absences*

These items (iii) to (vi) are fully covered in Chapter 2 and it is not intended to discuss them here. However, project leaders would do well to look at Table 8.2 on p.142 which gives a comparison between different companies operating flexible working within the UK, illustrating the flex and core bands, the debit/credit to be carried forward, time allowed off during core time in half days, and their arrangements for lunch breaks.

The importance of comparisons of this type lies in the competitive labour market situation in which many companies find themselves. Thus, if a local competitor in this market has been generous in respect of his fwh schemes in terms of the items (ii) to (vi), it would be foolish to ignore the significance of this on future labour recruitment and turnover. On the other hand, as in most situations, the final solution will tend to be a compromise involving other variables as well as these.

Communications with Employees

Notwithstanding the importance of consulting with representatives of the workforce (see page 103) the project leader/steering committee will need to consider carefully the method of communicating the whole subject of fwh to the employees. This will be particularly important where its introduction was initiated by management rather than as a result of a request from the workforce or a union. The importance of good communications cannot be over emphasised and the method to be adopted must be clearly defined. In several of the larger installations in the UK there has been an initial rejection of the concept by the employees, and this has been partly due to the way it was put over to them. Simplicity is the key here. It is easy for a project leader/steering committee to fall into the trap of considering the main principles of a scheme in great detail without giving sufficient thought to the need to inform employees of the basic principles. If this is not done, then the "grapevine" will take over and will soon distort the principles and procedures to a point where they become unrecognisable. The points that will need to be communicated to the workforce are:

1. A general appreciation of fwh — its advantages to employees and management. The general limitations must also be mentioned to ensure that flexible working is not interpreted as giving a complete freedom of choice of working arrangements.
2. The main reasons for the introduction of the scheme.
3. The main principles (i)–(vi) of the preceding section.
4. The need for an objective time recording system where it is to be applied for.
5. Any specific necessary limitations which will need to be imposed on individual departments or employees.

(i) *Communications with Management*
     Before this information is made known to the workforce the project leader/steering committee must ensure that all members of management are fully conversant with all aspects of the proposals. This is probably best communicated to management directly by individual or group discussion with time set aside for questions. If such a meeting is held the project leader/steering committee should be supported by at least one member of top management who will introduce the subject and at the same time indicate senior management's

commitment to it. The meeting should be so structured that, in addition to an information handout (see below), time should be set aside for questions and discussion.

This is most important for two reasons:

(a) To assess management's reaction — in some of the earlier experiments this was very mixed. Areas of apprehension are likely to arise in relation to the additional duties which may be imposed upon them in supervising the scheme, and also the problems which fwh can create in terms of work planning, and ensuring adequate supervisory and operational cover over the total bandwidth. These objections can best be met by pointing out that one of the basic concepts of fwh is that employees will accept a greater sense of responsibility for their work, and as a result require less direct supervision.

(b) To allow a discussion on the need for an objective time recording system which will be used by all. This will be resisted, in varying degrees, on the grounds that managers are task orientated and not given to clock watching. This special problem is discussed fully on page 94.

Other problems that should be raised at this meeting are those relating to possible contravention of legal implications, safety aspects, and effects on outside suppliers and customers. For those individual managers who have particular departmental problems they are best seen and consulted with subsequent to the main meeting, when there will be an opportunity to expand and air their difficulties. However, a word of warning! — Sweeping alterations to the main basic principles which would apply only to an individual department should be resisted whenever possible, otherwise a situation can arise where several different schemes are operating in one building and this can cause deep feelings of animosity between the staff. The main aim should always be to keep one common set of rules for all, but to accept that there will inevitably be some limitations on the amount of flexibility which can be afforded to certain individuals. The reasons for the limitations will need to be explained to those affected when the scheme is discussed with them.

It is very important that there is a handout available for distribution at the meeting so that everyone present has a copy of the proposals for the main principles of the scheme. The handout should be in a simple form, with examples of the likely effects of flexible working on the individual's balance between his private and working life. (A copy of a handout for distribution initially to management and, following their approval, to all employees is shown as Fig. 6.1).

At least one of the manufacturers of time recording equipment (Hengstler) has produced an introductory leaflet, outlining the main advantages of the scheme, but it is the view of the authors that this should be used with discretion. A well-prepared company handout is likely to prove much more acceptable.

(ii) *Communication with the Workforce*

Once the support of management and supervision has been gained then the next step will be to inform the workforce. This is probably best done through the departmental/group meeting led by the individual manager in the presence of either the project leader or a member of the steering committee who will ensure that the details given to the employees throughout the organisation are common, and that only correct information is passed on to them. The advisor's attendance will also help the manager in answering questions which arise. However, his greatest asset will be to assess the immediate response of the group to the scheme and to counsel them with a view to ensuring that the scheme will provide the benefits which were envisaged by the steering committee. The main objectives of the departmental meetings will be to obtain the support of the workforce and their commitment to a trial. There will be a need to ensure that the concept of fwh is thoroughly understood and that its advantages to the individual are made known. The handout (similar to the one mentioned above or suitably modified) will help to achieve the latter, and when it is distributed it is a good idea to stress that only the principles have been agreed at this stage; that these were drawn up for guidance and discussion only, and that they may change before the scheme is introduced. Also there should be a discussion on the type of recording system which is going to be used, and where possible a sample kit should be loaned from the suppliers for demonstration to the workforce.

The project leader must be prepared for the necessity of repeat meetings in certain circumstances. At all times the natural caution and conservatism of workforces towards management sponsored schemes should be appreciated. Work

113

Fig 6.1 : Example of a Handout for Employees Participating in an Initial Trial

FLEXIBLE WORKING HOURS

The underlying principle of flexible working hours ("Flextime") is quite simple. Fixed times of arrival at and departure from work are replaced by a working day which is split into two different "types" of time. The middle parts of the working day, called "core time", are the only periods when all employees must be at their job. The flexibility is at the beginning and end of the morning and afternoon each day. Thus, it is left to each individual to choose when to arrive and leave subject to some necessary limitations which are explained below.

It sounds simple, and it is. In the organisations which have adopted Flextime staff have found it a means of acquiring more personal freedom and responsibility, as well as gaining useful personal conveniences.

What then are the advantages?

You at Your Best — It is a fact of life that people are different. Some are better first thing in the morning and others take much longer to reach their peak form, irrespective of the time they awaken in the morning. Whatever type of person you are, Flextime gives you the opportunity to adjust your work hours to your own "rhythm". It is not just more convenient, it is also healthier and medical opinion supports the idea that Flextime reduces the stress and strain associated with working fixed hours every day.

Avoiding the Crush — With Flextime the old idea of "punctuality" disappears. You can decide the time of your arrival and departure within the flexible hours and avoid the stress and strain of the missed train or bus and the traffic jam. Yet another possible advantage is that it may reduce the cost of travel to work.

Your Own Personal Affairs — One of the great benefits of Flextime is that you have much more opportunity of planning your own free time and private life. Personal matters can be kept private for it is no longer necessary to ask for permission and give a reason for leaving work somewhat earlier. For example, you can get home early to pick up the children, go shopping when shops and supermarkets are less crowded, go to a football match without having to rush, and so on.

Time Off — With Flextime, time actually worked is measured and any excess hours worked voluntarily can be used for time off, taken by agreement with your supervisor.

Under normal circumstances everyone must be present during core time. Outside core time, the hours you work can be varied, providing that at the end of a "settlement period" which will probably be four weeks, the balance must not be more than five hours either way. Hours in excess of standard hours, i.e. a credit balance, can be taken as time off during the next settlement period. Alternatively, a debit balance must be made up.

During each "settlement period" an employee may build up sufficient credits to take one full half day off, providing, of course, that this is taken at a time convenient to his workload.

You will realise that in its detailed application Flextime is possible only to the extent that it is compatible with the essential operational requirements of our business. Where operations require team work, to ensure that operations are not interrupted, the whole team would need to conform to the decision of the majority. Experience has shown, however, that in practice

114

this is not unduly restrictive, although everyone must be prepared to accept some limitations.

Time Recording — No progressive organisation subscribes to control for control's sake, and insistence on punctuality (which can, with today's traffic conditions, often be achieved only at the cost of leaving wide margins for which no credit is forthcoming) can be much resented by staff. A free-for-all, on the other hand, soon turns into abuse. This dilemma is resolved where Flextime is in operation because insistence on punctuality (no one can be punctual if there is no precise moment of arrival to confirm to) is replaced by recording the number of hours worked. This is necessary with Flextime's opportunity for variation in daily working hours according to personal choice, for reconciliation of hours worked.

Old-style industrial time clocks and punch cards are becoming less and less used, but new types of time recorders specifically designed for Flextime are now available. They consist of individual counters which are linked to a remote master clock. Each employee is allocated a time counter and a personal coded key. When you arrive you insert your key into your own counter close to your place of work. It immediately starts to record your presence. When you leave you remove your key and the counter ceases to record time. Where, for some reason or another, you are working away from the building, special arrangements are made to record your hours. The same applies when you are away ill and are still eligible for payment. Since the recorders measure time cumulatively, there is no record, in the sense of a print-out on a clock card, of actual arrival and departure times and there is, of course, no reason why there should be. All that is recorded is your periods of attendance so that the "value" of your hours worked can be calculated.

Despite the benefits which can accrue to the individual employee by the variation of hours of commencing and finishing work, some individuals, however, may prefer to carry on working the same hours as at present - this is entirely possible within the framework of Flextime.

The Principles of the Scheme Proposed for the Company's Administrative Headquarters
The following proposals are put forward as an initial basis for further discussion only, and may be changed, dependent upon employees' views, before the experiment is introduced.

The Working Day

Start of work between	08.00 — 09.30
Finish work between	16.30 — 18.00
Flexible lunch break between	*12.30 — 14.00
Core time	09.30 — 12.30
Bandwidth	08.00 — 18.00
Contracted weekly attendance	37½ hours

*A minimum lunch break of 30 minutes must be taken and all lunch breaks must include the period of 13.00 hours to 13.30 hours.

If it is decided to go ahead with the trial a detailed handout will be given to each participant.

groups will not react similarly, even in identical situations, and a patient, understanding approach is necessary when resistance is met. However, assuming that the employees agree to a trial then they should be informed of the starting date.

(iii) *Exclusions*

Where the experiment is to be tried out in one or two departments then it will be necessary to inform those departments which have not been selected to participate in the trial and to give them the plans for its extension into their area, assuming the success of the experiment. If for any reason there are departments or persons for whom it is expected that flexible working would not be possible at any stage then they must be told as soon as feasible and the reasons for their exclusion explained to them. Consideration might be given to any compensatory benefits which could be afforded to them, although this is a matter on which opinions, at management level, are likely to be greatly divided.

Ordering and Installing the Equipment

Once the management and work force are committed to the trial then an order should be placed for the equipment and its installation planned. Where this is electrical or electronic, consultation with the installation engineer or electrician will be necessary and in the case of a computerised system then details of the plan will need to be arranged with the DP manager or systems analyst. Some manufacturers will provide their equipment on a rental basis during the trial, at the end of which the organisation has the opportunity to purchase and receives a rebate towards the capital cost, or total rental cost. The final decision to rent or buy can thus be deferred to a later stage.

Detailed Rules

As a result of their meetings with both management and employees the project leader/steering committee will now be in a position to draw up the detailed rules.

The amount of detail will vary from one organisation to another but will probably contain information relating to the following points:

   (i)   Arrangements for lunch break
 (ii) Arrangements for tea breaks (where applicable)
(iii) Instructions on time recording and use of
        equipment including the recording of absences
        (where applicable).
 (iv) Length of settlement period with dates of
        settlement periods for the trial
  (v) Reconciliation of hours worked against
        contracted hours
 (vi) Any limits to flexibility

Some organisations will probably choose to keep these rules relatively simple so that they are easily understood, thus giving managers some discretion as to the way the scheme will operate within their own department. Other organisations will feel the need for a very detailed set of rules covering all eventualities and this will probably be necessary where there is strong union involvement. Where they are detailed the readers' capabilities must be considered and they should be written in simple terms wherever possible. In some cases there will be a need for two sets of rules, one for distribution to the employees in a simplified form and the other a detailed rule book, kept by management, but available for inspection by an employee on request. Both the final rules and any changes in administration procedures will require discussion with management and employees before the scheme is started. (Problems concerning administration procedures are discussed in Chapter 5). In addition final preparations for the recording system are to be considered so that any forms or instructions concerning this aspect can be printed.

Copies of four sets of specimen rules are shown in Appendix I.

Monitoring the Trial

At this stage, and before the trial gets underway, consideration must be given to the form of monitoring which will need to be carried out during the trial period. This may consist of statistical information, that is, rates of casual absenteeism, employees work performance and spot checks on times of arrival or finish, etc.

Probably the best way to decide what information needs to be monitored is to establish what information will be necessary to evaluate the success or failure of the experiment at its conclusion. (This aspect is discussed in detail in Chapter 7).

The actual start of the trial will be a testing time for the project leader/steering committee who will need to watch it carefully to ensure that the rules are thoroughly understood and being correctly adhered to. Swift action must be taken to stamp out any discrepancies or abuses which occur and to settle any problems which are raised by both management and workforce.

For the scheme to be successful then follow-up of complaints and grievances must be given priority and settled quickly, otherwise the workforce will lose confidence and the trial will be a failure.

Attitude Survey

Towards the end of the trial the views of management and employees must be surveyed before any recommendation is made to senior management as to the success or failure of the scheme. This can be done informally through discussion, but is more likely to be objective if it is carried out by means of a questionnaire. However, before this is prepared the project leader/steering committee will need to consider the information which will be most helpful to them in evaluating the project.

The questions which will be asked in a questionnaire should include direct questions relating to whether or not the employee is in favour of the concept of fwh and any changes which he feels would improve the scheme. There should also be a number of indirect questions which not only serve to check the validity of the answers to the direct questions but also explore more deeply the whole area of fwh, and its effect on the employee's working/private life. A copy of a typical questionnaire is shown in Figure 6.2 and the results of several surveys are discussed in Chapter 8.

Management's view of the scheme might also be assessed by means of a questionnaire, but in the small-to medium-sized organisation this can be done by individual discussion. The project leader/steering committee may prefer the informal method since a more detailed view is likely to emerge and the long-term implications for management are more accurately assessed.

Fig 6.2 : A Typical Questionnaire for Assessing Employee Reaction to FWH.

Memo to: All Employees Participating in Flexible Working
              Hours Trial

Memo from: ....

Subject: Flexible Working Hours Questionnaire

In order that we can assess the success or failure of the F.W.H. trial, I
shall be grateful if you will tick the appropriate boxes and complete
the questionnaire below, posting it in the box provided in the Recep-
tion Area not later than ....
Thank you.

— —

1. Do you wish to continue to work 'flexible   YES ☐
    working hours'?   NO   ☐

2. Do you find 'flexible working hours' make
    your life:
    (a) Easier   ☐
    (b) The same as before   ☐
    (c) Harder   ☐
    (d) Do not know   ☐

3. What are the advantages of flexible hours to
    you personally?
    (a) Avoids morning and/or evening rush   ☐
    (b) Better balance between work and private life   ☐
    (c) Easier travel   ☐
    (d) Other (please specify) ....
         ....

4. Have you taken any complete half days off?   YES ☐
                                                   NO   ☐

5. What are the disadvantages to you, if any of flexible working
    hours?
    ....
    ....

6. What changes to the system would you suggest?
    ....
    ....

With the statistical information and the attitude surveys the project leader/steering committee will be in a position to consider and make recommendations to senior management for the continuation or rejection of flexible working and any changes which they think necessary to improve the scheme. So far the UK response has been most enthusiastic and many organisations have found it possible to extend their flexibility as the result of a successful experiment. As far as is known there has not been an organisation in the UK which has abandoned the scheme after the trial period, though there is a report of a West German company that did so.

A Step-by-Step Check List

A. *Feasability Study*
1. Decision by senior management to consider the introduction of an experimental scheme.
2. Senior management appoints a senior manager and/or project co-ordinator (in future called Project co-ordinator) to investigate and to introduce scheme.
3. Project co-ordinator informs unions of company's intentions.
4. Project co-ordinator researches past experience and knowledge, including if possible, a visit to an organisation operating fwh.
5. Project co-ordinator investigates varying types of recording equipment, their suitability, limitations and costs.
6. Project co-ordinator makes recommendations to senior management, which, if positive, may include a request for a steering committee. If a positive recommendation is accepted, then stage B is set in motion.

B. *Detailed Investigation and Recommendations*
1. Steering committee is set up and project co-ordinator informs it of experience gained so far.
2. Project co-ordinator/steering committee consider organisational needs through discussion and make recommendations to senior management on the main principles of the scheme, incorporating the following:
   (a) Length, scope and size of experiment — who will be included in the trial? Will it be the whole organisation or simply one or two departments — If it is the latter which ones? Proposed length of trial.

(b)   Type of recording system

(c)   Bandwidth — flexible and core times

(d)   Size of credit and debit carry over to next settlement period

(e)   Time allowed off in core time (half or whole days, credit leaves).

(f)   Treatment of overtime, medical/other absences.

(g)   Proposed method for communicating general appreciation of fwh and the outline principles to employees.

3.   Senior management agree to main principles of scheme including type of recording system to be used.

C.   *Communications and Discussions*

1.   Project co-ordinator prepares preliminary guide rules and, for distribution amongst employees, a handout explaining fwh and its advantages for employees.

2.   Project co-ordinator and steering committee discuss preliminary guide rules and proposed recording system with managers of departments to be included in the trial.

3.   Project co-ordinator discusses with relevant managers and supervisors, problems associated with individual departments. Supervision at extremes of bandwidths, necessary safety measures, legal implications, contacts with outside suppliers and customers are considered.

4.   Project co-ordinator, managers and employees' representatives discuss the proposed experiment *with the employees who will be involved,* and problems are reviewed.

D.   *Pre-trial Preparations*

1.   Project co-ordinator places final order for any equipment and plans its installation with engineer.

2.   Project co-ordinator informs other departmental heads of trial, and discusses with them any extensions to it which are envisaged and may affect them.

3.   Project co-ordinator and steering committee consider any necessary changes in administration procedures and prepare detailed rules and 'Guide Rules for Employees' (it may be desirable to issue a less detailed set of rules to employees which are easy to understand, provided that they have access to the full rule book).

4.   Project co-ordinator and steering committee discuss and

obtain agreement to detailed rules from senior management and unions.

5. Equipment is installed and tested.
6. 'Guide Rules for Employees' are issued to those participating in the trial, and the scheme and type of recording system is explained to them in detail.
7. Project co-ordinator/steering committee sets up a system for monitoring statistical information required during the trial.

E. *Monitoring the Trial and Recommendations*
1. Trial starts.
2. Project co-ordinator watches the trial carefully by taking positive steps to iron out any problems or discrepancies which occur.
3. Toward the conclusion of the trial project co-ordinator/ steering committee conduct an attitude survey to assess response to the scheme by employees, management and unions. If there is a desire for its continuation, then suggestions for any alterations to the rules are sought.
4. Project co-ordinator/steering committee consider and make recommendations to senior management on:
   (a) Suspension or continuation of the scheme.
   (b) Any modifications considered desirable, bearing in mind the results of the attitude survey conducted amongst the employees, the views of management and unions, and statistical information obtained during the trial.
   (c) Extension of the scheme into other departments.
5. Senior management accepts or rejects the recommendations prepared by the project co-ordinator/steering committee, and decisions taken by senior management are communicated to the employees who must again be given a full opportunity to discuss them.

7. An Exploratory Model

In a previous chapter the literature on the subject was surveyed, and a summary of the claimed advantages and disadvantages presented. These 'pros and cons' are not hard to find, but it is no exaggeration to say that the majority are speculative, emotive and impressionistic. Much of the writing emphasises the superficial perceptions of managers, trade unionists, consultants, recording equipment manufacturers and journalists as to how they 'see' the impact of a fwh system in a present or projected installation.

It is conceded that some hard data is available, based mainly on attitude surveys (see chapter 8) and some companies have genuinely attempted to produce figures on absenteeism, labour turnover, productivity and so on. Yet the sad fact is that, so far, the authors are aware of no systematic studies designed to produce, in statistically significant terms, some type of framework which could be used for cost-benefit analysis, both before and after installation. There is no doubt that such a framework would be useful.

The Need for an Exploratory Model

A model is needed that can be used for three purposes.
1. *Investigation*
   To help management investigate the probable effect of fwh in their own company.
2. *Design*
   To help management design a particular system of fwh which will enable the company to meet its objectives in installing such a system.
3. *Evaluation*
   To help management evaluate a system, once installed, and establish its relative effectiveness.

The three purposes are inter-related and this, conveniently, allows the development of a single framework for all three.

Fig 7.1 : Exploratory Model for FWH.

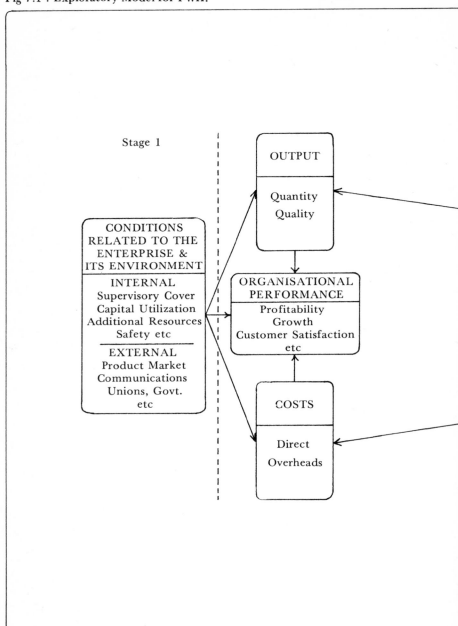

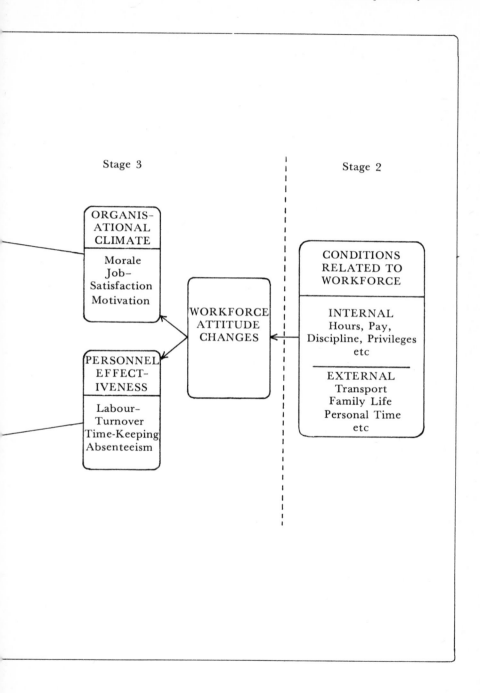

Stage 3

ORGANIS-
ATIONAL
CLIMATE

Morale
Job–
Satisfaction
Motivation

PERSONNEL
EFFECT-
IVENESS

Labour–
Turnover
Time-Keeping
Absenteeism

WORKFORCE
ATTITUDE
CHANGES

Stage 2

CONDITIONS
RELATED TO
WORKFORCE

INTERNAL
Hours, Pay,
Discipline, Privileges
etc

EXTERNAL
Transport
Family Life
Personal Time
etc

125

The Model
This is developed in three stages, and a broad outline of the elements in each stage are given in Figure 7.1. A framework of this type allows the investigation/design/evaluation to take place on a progressive basis. Consider the investigation, which would commence at Stage 1. If, at that stage, management is not satisfied with the probable impact of fwh, then there may be no need to proceed to Stage 2. Similarly, if the effects appear unfavourable at Stage 2, investigation at Stage 3 might not be necessary.

However, since the whole is often greater than the parts, the three stages must be analysed as an entity if the total systems effect is to be evaluated.

STAGE ONE (See Fig. 7.2)

The Enterprise in its Environment
Central to all our considerations is the enterprise in relation to its environment. The business enterprise is the characteristic institution of modern industrial society and, in the context used here, includes industrial, commercial, service, and administrative organisations, and has to be considered both in relation to its internal structure and its external environment.

The relationships between internal and external factors are shown in Figure 7.2. In investigation, design and evaluation, it is important to assess the impact of a fwh installation on both sets of factors, taking into account that changes in an internal factor will interact with one or more external factors. A practical preliminary investigation might proceed as follows, on a step by step basis, commencing with an evaluation of fwh on internal factors.

Internal Factors
Step 1   *Nature of Technology*
    (a)   What characteristic work patterns are imposed by technology on each work situation?
    (b)   What fwh configuration best meets the needs of that situation?
Step 2   *Work Procedures*
    (a)   What changes in work procedures are necessary, in each work situation, to accommodate fwh?
    (b)   What are the likely reactions from managers, supervisors and workforce to these changes?

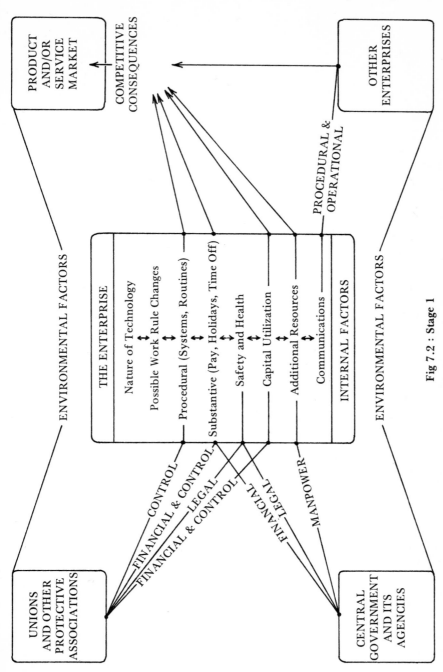

Fig 7.2 : Stage 1

PRODUCT AND/OR SERVICE MARKET

COMPETITIVE CONSEQUENCES

OTHER ENTERPRISES

ENVIRONMENTAL FACTORS

THE ENTERPRISE

Nature of Technology

Possible Work Rule Changes

Procedural (Systems, Routines)

Substantive (Pay, Holidays, Time Off)

Safety and Health

Capital Utilization

Additional Resources

Communications

INTERNAL FACTORS

ENVIRONMENTAL FACTORS

PROCEDURAL & OPERATIONAL

CONTROL

FINANCIAL & CONTROL

LEGAL

FINANCIAL & CONTROL

FINANCIAL

LEGAL

MANPOWER

UNIONS AND OTHER PROTECTIVE ASSOCIATIONS

CENTRAL GOVERNMENT AND ITS AGENCIES

127

Step 3   *Possible Modifications to Remuneration and Terms of Employment*
    (a)   How are contracts of employment going to be affected by fwh?
    (b)   What is the likely effect in terms of time-off, discipline, tea-breaks etc?
    (c)   Are there likely to be demands for more remuneration from all, or certain, groups of the workforce?

Step 4   *Capital Utilization*
    (a)   Will utilization of capital assets be affected by fwh?
    (b)   What restrictions on freedom of choice will be necessary to ensure that utilization of assets does not fall?
    (c)   How acceptable will these restrictions be to the workforce?

Step 5   *Safety and Health*
    (a)   How will legislation affect the application of fwh to certain occupational groups?
    (b)   What safety hazards could arise in a given fwh application?
    (c)   What will be the long term effect of fwh on the health of the workforce?

Step 6   *Additional Resources*
    (a)   Will extra supervision be required with the new system?
    (b)   Will additional resources be needed in the accounts section to deal with modified pay systems?
    (c)   Will additional labour be required to cover time-off in core time due to credit/debit leave units?
    (d)   Will extra staff be needed for fwh administration?

Step 7   *Communications*
    (a)   Will senior managers be available for meetings as and when required?
    (b)   How will lateral communication between functional departments be affected during flexible time bands?
    (c)   To what extent does the internal communication system depend upon a central work station (e.g. a switchboard)?

External factors
So far, we have only considered those factors which are internal

to the enterprise. Let us now look at those factors external to the situation which are likely to be affected by (or are likely to affect) the installation of a flexible working hour system in the organisation.

Step 8   *Trade Unions and Staff Associations*

(a)   What is the background; conflict and agression or cooperation?

(b)   What attitudes are unions or staff associations likely to adopt?

(c)   What type of strategies are they likely to use?

(d)   At what stage (if at all) should they be invited into discussions?

Step 9   *Employers' Associations*

(a)   To what extent will the action be approved/disapproved by the association?

(b)   What reaction is this likely to produce among fellow members of the association; and on their relationships with their employees?

(c)   What are the likely consequences of the various outcomes in (a) and (b) with regard to the position of the enterprise.

Step 10   *Customer Response*

(i)   Communication and Procedures

(a)   Will our customers accept that all managers are available only during core time?

(b)   Will our suppliers accept the new procedures which we are using because of the introduction of the system?

(c)   Will our associates (group headquarters, sister companies, overseas agencies) accept the communication constraints and procedural changes?

(d)   Will the system affect our method of distribution if this is handled by an outside company?

(ii)   Competitive Consequences

(a)   To what extent, in general, will our competitive position in the product market be affected?

Moving to a more specific line of approach, one would have to ask:

(b)   What will be the competitive consequences in

a particular product market, given a particular configuration of flexible working hours and a particular group of competitors.

Step 11   *Central Government and its Agencies*

(a) To what extent are statutory minimum wage requirements likely to be affected by changes in internal factors (say by changes in substantive rules — remuneration, time-off etc)?

(b) To what extent is the Factories Inspectorate likely to be concerned in changes in the structure of the working day for all employees or for particular groups of employees.

(c) To what extent is the Department of Employment likely to be involved in possible increases/decreases in manpower resources?

(The last named might arise if changes in work procedure had to be adopted which affected manning levels.)

Summary of the First Stage

It can be seen that a very lengthy investigation is possible at this stage. No attempt has been made to produce an exhaustive list of questions and, indeed, those postulated are offered as guide-lines for thinking rather than as absolute yard-sticks.

How detailed the investigation is to be will depend upon the ability of the enterprise to elaborate its requirements in terms of the internal and external factors. Only if, at this stage, does it appear that the impact of the system is likely to produce a positive effect, should the manager proceed to the second stage, which is now discussed.

STAGE 2 (See Fig. 7.3)

In Stage 1 we have been concerned, in general terms, with the impact of a flexible working scheme on the enterprise. In Stage 2 it is necessary to establish how the workforce will be affected by the introduction of such a scheme.

Changes in Conditions

Broadly speaking, the impact of a flexible working hour system will affect the condition of the workforce both *inside* and *outside* the enterprise.

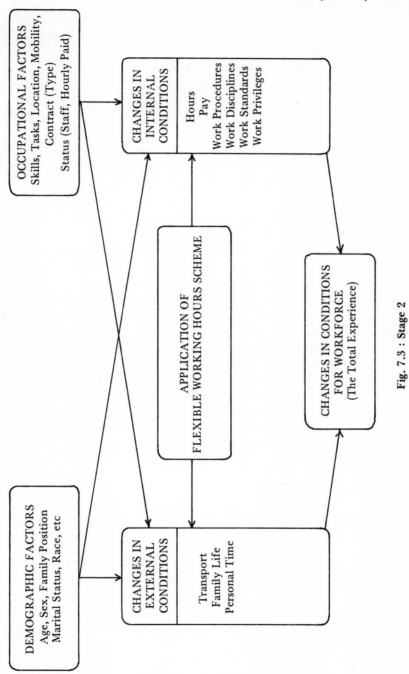

OCCUPATIONAL FACTORS
Skills, Tasks, Location, Mobility, Contract (Type)
Status (Staff, Hourly Paid)

CHANGES IN INTERNAL CONDITIONS

Hours
Pay
Work Procedures
Work Disciplines
Work Standards
Work Privileges

DEMOGRAPHIC FACTORS
Age, Sex, Family Position Marital Status, Race, etc

CHANGES IN EXTERNAL CONDITIONS

Transport
Family Life
Personal Time

APPLICATION OF FLEXIBLE WORKING HOURS SCHEME

CHANGES IN CONDITIONS FOR WORKFORCE
(The Total Experience)

Fig. 7.3 : Stage 2

Effect on External Conditions　These are the conditions enjoyed by the workforce external to the enterprise. They would include, among others —
  (i) Changes in transportation patterns,
 (ii) Changes in personal time utilization,
(iii) Changes in family life.

Effect on Internal Conditions　These are the conditions and rewards enjoyed by the workforce within the enterprise. They would include, among others —
  (i) Hours of work
 (ii) Monetary rewards
(iii) Work procedures
(iv) Work standards
 (v) Work disciplines
(vi) Work privileges
At a very general level it is immediately obvious that a change in the structure of the working day is bound to affect every individual in the enterprise, to a greater or lesser degree, and that each individual's external and internal conditions will be modified in some way.This, however, is too abstract a proposition. The average worker does not exist. Each individual will be concerned with the impact of the system on *his* conditions, or on the conditions of *his* work group. The problem, therefore, is to identify these changes, in terms of individual workers, or, if the organisation is a large one, in terms of homogeneous groups of workers who will be affected in broadly similar ways.

Breakdown of Workforce
The factors which can be used in isolating individuals and groups are demographic and occupational.

Demographic Factors　These are the variables which are used to separate out communities on the basis of:
　　Age
　　Sex
　　Marital Status
　　Family Position
　　Race　　　　　　etc

132

Occupational Factors These are the variables which are used to separate out workforces on the basis of:

Skills
Occupations
Tasks
Location
Mobility
Contract (Full Time/Part Time)
Status (Staff/Hourly Paid) etc.

Every individual in the enterprise can be allocated to a group whose boundaries can be pre-determined by parameters selected from the above demographic and occupational factors.

The definition of these groups must be sufficiently precise to enable significant variations in system effect to be identified and measured while, at the same time, it must not fragment the workforce to a point where the number of groups becomes ridiculously high and variations in effect, between them, lose their significance. Some compromise must be struck between the desire to account for *ali* changes in conditions as they affect each and every individual and the need to see individuals as members of fairly well defined demographic and occupational groups.

The very real problems involved in an evaluation of this type are illustrated by the following example:

Consider a Packaging Department under the control of a Manager, 4 Supervisors and 40 Packers. There are two separate packaging operations; product packaging (on conveyor lines) and dispatch packaging (in the warehouse).

Here it is possible to identify 4 main occupational groups, in volved in management, supervision, product packaging and dispatch packaging, yet many of the skills and duties in one group are common to another. For example, the skills and duties of supervision overlap with those of more senior management. The same might be said of packaging.

If we now consider some of the other factors, we begin to appreciate the complexity of the problem. For example, some of the packers may be women. Some may be married with children; some may have no dependent children. Some may be full-time, some part-time. Some may travel to work in a husband's or friend's car, some may use public transport.

Thus, although the packaging department may appear to be a homogeneous group in terms of location, work task and interdependability, there is no substance to the concept of the 'average packaging worker'. Yet, if he is to make progress, the assessor must proceed at a fairly general level, in terms of occupational and work groups, (introducing demographic factors where necessary), and attempt to evaluate the different sets of reaction to the plan.

It would be possible to proceed with such an assessment on the following step by step basis.

Step 1   *Identify Occupational Groups*
         Allocate the workforce to various occupational and/or task groupings.

Step 2   *Internal Effects*
         Attempt to obtain answers to the following questions:
         (a)   *How, in general, will each group be affected within the organisation?*
         (b)   *How, in particular, will each group be affected in terms of —*
                        Work procedures?
                        Overall earnings?
                        Traditional privileges?
                        Organisational discipline?

Step 3   *Identify Demographic Groups*
         Allocate the workforce to various demographic groupings (note, it is possible for an individual to be in more than one demographic group).

Step 4   *External Effects*
         Attempt to obtain answers to the following questions:
         (a)   *How, in general, will each group be affected outside the organisation?*
         (b)   *How, in particular, will each group be affected in terms of —*
                        Patterns of transportation?
                        Utilization of personal time?
                        Family life?

If it appears that, in general, the workforce, (or sub-groups of the workforce) will perceive improvements in their material conditions (both internal and external to the enterprise), then it will be possible to pass to the final stage of the analysis in Stage 3.

STAGE 3

In Stage One we attempted to evaluate the changes which would take place within the enterprise and in the relationships between

134

the enterprise and the various sectors of its operating environment. In Stage Two we attempted to predict the changes which would take place in the conditions of the workforce both internal and external to the enterprise. It is now necessary, in the third and final stage of the evaluation, to predict the effect of these changes on the performance of the enterprise, and the argument can best be followed by referring back to Figure 7.1.

Enterprise Performance
The criteria of performance will depend upon the nature of the enterprise. Various indices can be used, for example:
    Profitability
    Return on capital
    Customer satisfaction
    Long-term growth
    Service to the public
Whatever index of performance is chosen (and this will vary widely between local authority department, public company and nationalized industry) performance is bound to be affected by output and cost.

Output and Costs
Whether we are concerned with a product or service, it should be possible to quantify output in terms of *quantity* and *quality*, and providing that standards for the latter have been established in definitive terms, measurements of these variables (or, more precisely, predictions regarding possible changes following the introduction of a scheme) should present few problems.

    Costs may be a little more difficult to establish, since there often appear to be problems of definition and accountants themselves vary in their approach as to how the unit cost of a product or service might be computed. Many, in fact, would challenge the usefulness of unit cost, regarding it as an outmoded and imprecise concept, unless qualified in terms of production levels and allocation of overheads. Nevertheless, costs *are* established *and* allocated in on-going enterprises and if the method varies between organisations this matters little within the confines of a particular enterprise.

RELATIONSHIP BETWEEN STAGE 2 AND PERFORMANCE

The Effect of Attitude Changes
It has long been known that the attitudes of workforces are affected

by the conditions they enjoy both internal and external to the enterprise. It is conceivable, therefore, that the introduction of a flexible working hour scheme would change attitudes and, hopefully, that this would lead to improvements in organizational climate, and personal effectiveness.

Organisational Climate
Definitions of this concept vary, but organisational climate would be regarded as good when
> morale is high
> there is job satisfaction
> the workforce is highly motivated

These concepts are difficult to measure precisely, yet these are the very areas where, if morale *is* high and the workforce *is* motivated strongly the level of output is immediately affected in terms of quantity and quality. Thus, if the introduction of a scheme changes attitudes in such a way that the organisational climate improves, we can anticipate improvements in output which will raise company performance.

Personnel Effectiveness
This is considered to be high when
> absenteeism is low
> time-keeping is good
> labour turnover is low

Favourable changes in attitude, following the introduction of a scheme, should lead to high personnel effectiveness with resultant indirect reductions in costs through reduced absenteeism and better timekeeping. At the same time, direct savings should follow through reduced recruitment, training and induction costs.

RELATIONSHIP BETWEEN STAGE 1 AND PERFORMANCE

The Effect of Enterprise Changes
Finally, it would be necessary to re-examine the changes which would arise within the enterprise and within those sectors of the environment with which the enterprise makes contact, so that an evaluation could be made of the likely effect of these changes on company performance.

The Indirect Effect
Such changes could have an indirect effect; for example, it is possible

Fig. 7.4 : Effect of FWH Scheme on Organisational Performance

BALANCE SHEET

How are the following criteria of performance
PROFITABILITY: RETURN ON CAPITAL:
GROWTH: GOODWILL: SERVICE TO PUBLIC
affected by

DEBIT	CHANGES TO THE ENTERPRISE	CREDIT
	Direct Effect	
	.... Output	
	...................Costs	
	Indirect Effect	
	.............Customer Goodwill.............	
	............Approval of Society.............	
	CHANGES TO THE WORKFORCE	
	Organisational Climate	
	.... Morale	
	.... Motivation	
	.... Job Satisfaction	
	PERSONNEL EFFECTIVENESS	
	Indirect Effect	
	.... Labour Turnover.............	
	...............Time Keeping...............	
	.... Absenteeism...............	
	Direct Effect	
	.... Recruitment Costs.............	
	.... Induction Costs.............	
	.... Training Costs..............	

that a client might be dissatisfied by the fact that he could now only be sure of contacting the marketing manager during core time, with the result that goodwill (and sales) could be lost and company performance would fall.

The Direct Effect (Output and Costs)

On the other hand, the changes could have a direct effect on output and/or costs. For example the need for additional resources to operate flexible working hours could increase costs and *reduce* company performance. On the other hand, reductions in overtime working subsequent to the introduction of a scheme might reduce costs and *increase* company performance. Increased asset utilization might follow the introduction of the scheme, with resulting increase in output. On the other hand, communication problems (internal and external) subsequent to an installation, might cause a fall in output with a resultant fall in company performance.

Some sort of balance sheet might be attempted in order to establish whether changes in the enterprise would affect company performance favourably or unfavourably. The Balance Sheet (shown as Fig. 7.4) is, in fact, a form of question and answer, in which the nature of the response will determine whether the item is a debit or a credit.

It may not be possible to quantify answers to many of these questions, but an attempt must be made, if only on an approximate basis, to allocate values to each of the parameters.

This, in turn, depends upon a step by step analysis, as described in Stages 1 and 2. Without this logical approach, estimates become guesses and the whole process becomes valueless. The use of a model of this type may appear at worst tedious and at best rather imprecise, yet without it management have no tool to evaluate work week restructuring. It is hoped that it will prove of some use to those who wish to carry out preliminary investigation and/or installation evaluation of fwh schemes as applied to their own organisation.

8. Organisational Experience with F.W.H.

Details of particular applications of fwh schemes are of interest and, as with many other management innovations, most organisations appear to be eager to publicise their experience. Much can be gained from reading these company reports since they often identify pitfalls and problems, in addition to summarising attitudes to the system before and after an installation. Many of these reports are written following post-installation surveys conducted by management, usually through the personnel department.

Post Installation Surveys

The majority of surveys in this category appear to be of a relatively simple type and appear to be mainly concerned with establishing the workforces' degree of satisfaction with the scheme, their perceptions of its benefits and suggestions for changes for improvement. A questionnaire of this type, used by Riker laboratories, Loughborough, is shown on page 119 and an analysis of a survey (using a slightly modified questionnaire) carried out at one of their factories towards the end of the trial period, is given (See Table 8.1). This analysis, is best studied in relation to the 'Flexible Working Rules' used by Riker and these can be found on pages 157-160.

Some organisations have used a much more comprehensive questionnaire which not only ensures that more information is generated but that this data can be analysed in relation to various sub-groups within the organisation. Nevertheless, these sophisticated surveys are still concerned with only a few basic areas.

    (a)   Personal data
    (b)   Changes in working hour patterns
    (c)   Perceived advantages
    (d)   Recommendations for change,

and it seems to the authors that the majority of organisations will find the short questionnaire more than adequate for their purpose.

Table 8.1 : Analysis of Questionnaires Completed by Employees of Riker Laboratories (Dishley Factory) Towards the Conclusion of the Trial

Question	No.of Employees	%
1. Do you wish to continue to work Flexible Working Hours?		
YES:	156	97.5
NO:	3	1.9
DON'T KNOW:	1	.6
2. Do you find Flextime makes your life:		
(a) Easier	133	83.1
(b) Same as before	21	13.1
(c) Harder	4	2.5
(d) Don't know	2	1.3
3. What are the Advantages of Flextime to you Personally?		
(a) Avoids am/pm rush	31	19.4
(b) Better balance between work and private life	111	69.4
(c) Easier travel	31	19.4
4. Do you leave at 3.30 on Friday Afternoons?		
(a) As often as I can	60	47.6
(b) Sometimes	40	31.7
(c) Never	26	20.7
5. Have you taken any complete Half Days off?		
YES:	99	61.9
NO:	61	38.1

External Surveys

These surveys are likely to be of more value to the reader in helping him assess the general impact of fwh on organisations and, in particular, they allow trends and tendencies to be identified. These have significance at a national level. For example, it is important for a personnel manager in a British firm to know something of the UK experience. His counterpart, in Hamburg or Cologne, on the other hand, would be interested in the German experience.

Surveys of this type are much more searching than the in-company type described above and are concerned with much wider issues. In an attempt to gather information with which to synthesize organisational experience the authors carried out such a survey in March 1973. In this case, 36 organisations were sent a four-part questionnaire and a summary of the answers gives an interesting picture of the British experience.

PART 1

The first section attempted to generate information about the actual 'mechanics' of fwh; for example, were patterns beginning to emerge in terms of length of core-time, type of lunch break (flexible or fixed), time-off allowed per settlement period, and so on? A summary of these findings is shown in Table 8.2. A word of explanation is necessary. Column 2 describes the particular factor which, in the survey, appeared to be most popular. Column 3 describes the smallest (or shortest) value being used for the factor and Column 4 the greatest (or longest) value being used.

One interesting fact which emerges is the popularity of the 2 hour sequence as applied to morning flextime, morning core time, afternoon core time and evening flextime. Another interesting sidelight was the wide variance in credit carryover (2hrs to 30 hrs) reflecting the caution of some organisations and the high trust level of others. A surprisingly large number of companies (25%) offered employees the facility of an unlimited number of half-days off, provided that they were in credit. One company, when challenged that this might lead to a four day week development, admitted that, with some employees, this was already taking place; but that they were satisfied that the company's performance was not being impaired.

141

Table 8.2

F.W.H. Factor	Most Popular			Smallest		Greatest	
	%	hrs	Range	hrs	Range	hrs	Range
A.M. Flex Band	56	2	0800-1000	¼	0845-0900	2	0800-1000
A.M. Core Band	38	2	1000-1200	1½	1000-1130	3¼	0815-1230
P.M. Core Band	38	2	1400-1600	1	1500-1600	3	1300-1600
P.M. Flex Band	38	2	1600-1800	1	1630-1730	3	1600-1900
Lunch periods	75		Flexible		½ hr		unspecified
Max^m Credit Carry-over per settlement period	38		10 hrs		2 hrs		30 hrs
Max^m Debit Carry over per settlement period	31		10 hrs		2 hrs		10 hrs
No. of half-days settlement period	31		2		nil		unlimited
Types of time recording	75		meters		An equal split between clock card and manual systems		

PART 2

This section examined attitudes prior to installation and the steps taken to involve the workforce and unions (where applicable).

(a) *Initiative in Introducing fwh*

It appears that the majority of fwh schemes (82 per cent) were introduced on the basis of management initiative, triggered by articles read in the press or management journals. On the other hand, employee initiative was only responsible for 18 per cent of the installations.

(b) *Reasons for introducing fwh*

Of the many reasons given for introducing the scheme, the

142

most popular are undoubtedly travelling problems, the improvement of working conditions and the desire to give employees more personal freedom.

(c) *Management Doubts and Reservations*
Management reservations were initially expressed in 72 per cent of the installations, but in only 3 installations did this embrace 60 per cent or more of management involved. Greatest fears were expressed about the problems of supervisory cover at the extremes of the bandwidth.

(d) *Use of Consultants*
Only two organisations found it necessary to enlist the aid of a consultant (and in neither case was this bona fide outside help), but more than 50 per cent received aid from other firms. This confirms the views of the authors regarding installations, which is that much advice is available from outside the organisation if it is sought. Whether or not money might be saved by employing a consultant is not, however, yet established and in some cases help of this type might, in the long term, produce cost benefits.

(e) *Negotiations and Consultations*
Only three of the organisations found it necessary to have exploratory discussions with trade unions, although four had talks with staff associations. On the other hand eleven had discussions with their workforce (two companies talking to unions *and* workforce). It is impossible to draw significant conclusions about this, since no information was sought to establish exactly how many union and non-union organisations were in the sample. However, there may be a tendency for installations to take place in non-unionised and/or good labour relations situations and this appears to be borne out by the fact that, in almost all cases, the talks were of a consultative nature and no hard bargaining was reported.

PART 3

This section sought information about pilot schemes which had been operated prior to full installation of fwh schemes.

(a) *Pilot Schemes* (here defined as trial installations covering all, or a fraction, of the employees).

Pilot schemes were seen as necessary by 62 per cent of the organisations, and of those using pilot schemes, 50 per cent operated the trial with one fifth of the total staff. There appeared to be no clear trend in the type of departments chosen for pilot schemes and the number of departments covered ranged from three to six.

(b) *Evaluation of pilot schemes*
The universal method of evaluation was the questionnaire and all of the organisations operating a pilot scheme used this. In addition a variety of other methods were used by four of the organisations; (consultations, meetings, discussions etc).

(c) *Modification of ground rules*
Surprisingly, the great majority of organisations only found it necessary to make marginal alterations to their rules, following a trial period. This could indicate that, where a logical and consistent procedure has been followed in the first drafting of the ground rules, the project leader and his steering committee (see Chapter 6) can reasonably anticipate the needs of the workforce in a fwh scheme.

PART 4

This final section was concerned with management attitudes to fwh in the light of their experience, and the particular problems which they identified with the scheme.

(a) *Management attitudes after experience with fwh*
Eleven of the organisations attempted to evaluate management attitudes and again, the questionnaire was the most popular method, although alternative and/or complementary methods were also used. All respondents were asked to evaluate their management's attitudes on a ranking scale and these seemed to fall between enthusiastic and satisfied. In no case was management attitudes classed as dissatisified or very dissatisfied.

(b) *Particular Problems*
Very few problem areas were identified. The most common were in the service units (post, telephonists etc) and a question

which appeared in one organisation related to the extent to which managers should be involved in the scheme (For a full discussion of this see Chapter 5).

External surveys, of this type, are of particular value in that they identify trends and practices which have found favour in installations in Britain. The survey described above is of an exploratory nature, and more comprehensive and sophisticated surveys will no doubt be mounted to investigate the entire effect of work week restructuring on the individual, the manager, the organisation and society as a whole.

What has so far emerged is that applications are being handled imaginatively and boldly and that while strong patterns are evident in installations in Britain, organisations are taking the opportunity, where applicable, of experimenting widely in order to develop a scheme which fits their particular situation.

9. Trade Union Attitudes to F.W.H.

The attitudes of trade unions and other protective associations must be of interest to those considering the installation of a fwh scheme. There is an argument that trade unions in the UK tend to be highly conservative in their approach to innovation and change. It is not surprising then, to find that in the current literature on the topic, the majority are being labelled at best as reluctant to commit themselves, and at worst, as firmly opposed to fwh.

This reluctance of trade unions to take a more comprehensive approach to what they regard as their members' interests, has often been commented upon, but this does not mean that trade unions automatically oppose change. Trade unions, like other protective organisations, tend to react to situations as they arise and it is often difficult to predict the type of reaction on the basis of some generalisation about ideology or historical development of unions.

Thus, it is necessary to examine each issue as it develops, and it is the intention, in this chapter, to look specifically at statements and actions of British trade unions in relation to a specific innovation — flexible working hours. If general conclusions can be drawn, this will be done on the basis of such specific data as is available and not upon vague precepts about how unions react to change.

Experience in West Germany

It has been claimed that there has been complete cooperation between unions and employers in West Germany where, from the outset, German trade unions have been extensively involved in the installation of fwh schemes. This view finds support in a report by Bolton[1] who quotes the experience of DAG, the German Union of Administrative Employees (Deutsche Angestelltenge-werkschaft). This union published a brochure in 1970 which laid down guide lines for discussions with management on the introduction of fwh schemes. This approach, which is at once positive, unequivocal and definitive, is what one has come to expect when highly professional trade unions are confronted with

146

suggestions from management for innovation and change.

It would, however, be easy to idealise the German experience. Trade unions in West Germany can be just as protective and restrictive as their British counterparts. Very little precise information is available but there is some evidence that, in the early stages of its introduction in West Germany, Gleitzeit (literally, gliding time (fwh)) did encounter some opposition. Thus Hart-Davies [2] reports "opposition from the unions (considerable at first), has virtually died out, only the Metal Workers Union continuing to resist . . .". This view is confirmed by Deeson [3] who also claims continuing resistance by the Chemical Workers Union. Finally, the claim that unions in Germany, despite initial opposition, are having to respond to demands for fwh by their members, is argued by Bolton [4], tending to confirm that the situation in that country is a developing one.

Experience in the UK

The position in the UK may very well be similar to that which pertained in West Germany a few years ago. Certainly, the actual position is difficult to define. There is no lack of reports which, in the most speculative manner (and often on the basis of little supporting evidence), attempt to present the attitude of the British trade union movement to fwh. It is true that there is little evidence of general commitment by the trade union movement to policy statements on the innovation, but this should not be taken as necessarily implying opposition.

A Survey of British Trade Unions

In the absence of hard data, the authors decided to conduct a survey of the major TUC affiliated trade unions in Britain, with a view to obtaining definitive information about attitudes and involvement with fwh. A questionnaire was designed with the intention of establishing —
(a) How many unions had been involved in negotiations on fwh schemes and the extent and nature of that involvement.
(b) How many unions had issued major policy statements and/or guide lines to their members.
(c) The attitudes of trade unions to fwh in the general context of terms and conditions of employment.

32 trade unions were selected from sixteen of the eighteen trade and occupational groups of the TUC. These were chosen purely on the grounds of size (that is, the largest unions in each group were chosen) on the assumption that these were the more important of the unions in each group. No questionnaires were sent to non-TUC affiliated unions as these tend to be small and less easily identified.

ANALYSIS OF RESULTS

(a) *How many unions have been involved in negotiations ?*
Only five of the unions replying claimed to have been involved in negotiations in any way, and it is probably significant that all of these unions operate in the white-collar field.

One of the unions had been invited to take part in negotiations and had refused.

The other four had participated in negotiations; sometimes on the basis of a request by them (the unions) and sometimes on the basis of an invitation by the company.

(b) *The nature of negotiation and consultation*
The union which had refused did so on the grounds that they saw fwh as cutting across their alternative claim for *reduced* working hours. It may very well be, therefore, that this union has not rejected fwh as a feasible concept in the future; merely that, at the moment, it is not prepared to be tactically involved in discussing a proposed change in conditions of employment which might weaken the case for its main objective; the reduction of the work week.

The other unions who have participated in negotiations take the general view that, as the fwh concept affects terms of employment, then its proposed introduction is covered by existing procedure agreements. The unions do not, therefore, anticipate making 'requests' to be included in consultations and/or negotiations, but would expect to be approached automatically. This, in fact, has already taken place in a number of pilot schemes now being conducted and the unions claim that they have been as heavily involved in negotiations as they would be in any other discussions with employers.

Association of Scientific Technical and Managerial Staffs (ASTMS)
The attitude of ASTMS has been unique, among unions, in

their approach to fwh. The Insurance Staffs Section of this union, representing some 45,000 of the union's quarter of a million membership has been particularly active in this field and the pattern of initiative and negotiation, which has led to agreements being concluded with five insurance companies and covering 20,000 employees, typifies this uniqueness. In total, ASTMS has now obtained fwh agreements with six companies, these being—

    Pilkingtons Ltd.

    London & Manchester Assurance Co

    Liverpool Victoria Friendly Society

    Prudential Assurance Co

    Pearl Assurance Co

    Royal Insurance Co

The pattern of negotiations is described by Maurice Reynolds, National Secretary of the Insurance Staffs Section, ASTMS [5] when talking of the first fwh agreement concluded by the union

"Early in 1972, the subject of Flexible Working Hours was discussed by the Insurance Section of ASTMS and particular interest was shown by certain members in London & Manchester. In July 1972 the first tentative approach was made to the management of that company who expressed considerable interest. ASTMS supplied material on agreements in Germany and this country and the company agreed to the setting up of a small working party consisting of the General Manager and Data Processing Manager on one side, and the senior ASTMS lay official (London & Manchester) and myself on the other.

The report was produced within one month and in August was accepted by ASTMS members at a meeting and confirmed by the London & Manchester Board of Directors. The agreement was signed at the end of September and flextime commenced early in October.

The matter was reviewed in February, 1973 when there was full agreement that flextime had been an outstanding success".

It is interesting to note the very positive role played by the union in this case. The initiative appears to have come from ASTMS and its members. It was the union which opened negotiations, prepared background material and asked for a working party to be set up. Once the machinery was established the report was produced quickly; referred back to ASTMS members and company directors; a formal agreement was signed in September; and finally, approximately three months after the initial approach, a fwh trial scheme commenced.

A Company-Union Agreement on fwh
The agreement between London & Manchester Assurance Company Ltd, and ASTMS is not without interest, since it is probably one of the first comprehensive agreements of this type to be signed in Britain. It is reproduced as Appendix II and those likely to become involved in management-union negotiations on fwh would do well to study it closely.

(c) *Policy and Other Statements*
Only one union had issued a policy statement as such, to its members. This opposed fwh on the grounds that the unions has never agreed that hours worked in excess of normal hours should be balanced by time-off. They also objected to the use of recording devices.

Some unions obviously contemplate issuing policy statements, and many have produced considerable literature for their members to read. Most of these articles are printed in the union journals, and the overwhelming majority take a neutral line [6] , confining themselves to a description of the system with potted versions of advantages and disadvantages. Only one union has used its union journal to publish an article which is openly hostile to fwh [7]

Trade Union Congress (TUC)
As the supreme advisory body, co-ordinating the activities of some 142 affiliated trade unions, the TUC has considered the question of fwh, and in November 1972 the General Council issued a policy document [8], on Flexible Work Time. This five page document sets out brief details of the mechanics of fwh but is mainly concerned with pointing out possible disadvantages for trade unionists. These tend to be similar to those identified by TASS, but in addition there are claims that fwh schemes could help the employer by improving the efficiency of use of labour and capital resources. The document does, however, attempt to identify advantages as well

as disadvantages. Thus, in claiming that limitations on credit hour carryover is designed to protect the employer, it concedes that this could be in the workers' interest by countering pressure to extend holidays at the expense of increasing the working week. (The TUC's interest in reducing the working year for the British labour force is evident here). Similarly it accepts that, while for some workers' overtime earnings may be lost, for others, (particularly 'staff' workers whose extra time worked at the request of the employer has never been paid for) the scheme could ensure that they were compensated.

In conclusion, the document implies that a decision as to whether fwh is acceptable must be left to the workers involved; that the principles are innocuous enough but that the employer's motives must be examined carefully and installations continually monitored; and that effective negotiations depend upon a clear sighted appraisal of all the circumstances.

(d) *The General Attitudes of Trade Unions to fwh*
The analysis above indicates that perhaps too gloomy a view has been presented of trade union attitudes to fwh in the UK. Certainly there is no evidence of unions imposing an embargo on discussions between themselves and employers. The rather negative attitude adopted by one [7], and the equivocal statements of the TUC do not, at any stage, suggest a rejection of the concept. Rather do they, in the former case, seek to arm the union negotiators with ammunition, which can be used in the traditional 'protective' manner of the British trade union movement, and in the latter case, seek to establish an image of the 'let's be fair', 'two sides to every question', *reasonable* trade union movement.

In our survey it was evident that, where unions had rejected the concept of fwh for their members they had done so, not on the basis of a dogmatic ideological creed, but on what they perceived to be purely practical grounds. The most recurring theme was that of work technology and the following comments, by unions who claimed that they are unlikely to be involved, illustrate this:

Post Office Management Staffs Association: The operational character of our member's work (24 hours per day, 7 days per week) already has inbuilt flexibility in working hours.

National Union of Insurance Workers: Vast majority of members have freedom to work hours which suit them and policy holders best.

Confederation of Health Service Employees: Members mainly in hospital services where 24 hour coverage required. Shift systems are the norm and local branches arrange these to suit the circumstances.

National Union of Textile and Allied Workers: Do not contemplate involvement due to the variety of shift systems involved.

It would, of course, be most encouraging and conclusive if one could predict that, where the work technology did not cut across the concept, unions would all be as positive and accommodating as, for example, ASTMS. Unfortunately, it is not possible to make such a prediction. This is not because some unions are 'different' from other unions but that, in the weighing process which unions involve themselves in, when called upon to assess the merits and demerits of a management innovation on behalf of their members, certain unions have found themselves (given *their* situation — given *their* members work technology) coming down in favour of fwh schemes. It could very well be that, given a new situation, unions now in favour could come down just as heavily against the concept.

(e) *Likely patterns of negotiations*
It does appear, therefore, that management representatives consulting with trade unions on fwh are likely to be met with a pragmatic approach which would not be dissimilar to the attitude one would expect from unions confronted with *any other* management innovation. What is clear, however, is that there is little evidence of rejection of the concept on ideological grounds. Nor is there evidence, at this stage, that unions intend to use fwh installations to help them in their fight for a shorter working week, or to obtain additional financial rewards for their members, although obviously, management will be watching this closely.

It appears that the majority of unions will wish to be involved, from the outset, in all discussions leading up to an installation and will wish to secure the position of their members by means of a formal agreement on mutually acceptable ground rules.

This procedure is not new to management and unions in British industry and commerce and both sides are well equipped to handle these aspects.

(1) Bolton, J.H.   *Flexible Working Hours* Anbar Publications 1971 p.47
(2) Hart Davis D.   *Sunday Telegraph* 27th February 1972
(3) Deeson, A.F.L. *Works Management* July/August/1972 p.3.
(4) Bolton, J.H.   *Management Today* January 1973 p.33.
(5) Reynolds, M.   *Transcript of Unpublished Speech at I.P.M.*
                      Conference April 1973 — Supplied by Mr. Reynolds
(6) A.P.E.X.   *Topics Vol. 1* No.2 February 1973
(7) T.A.S.S.   *TASS News* 8th December 1972
(8) T.U.C.   *Flexible Work Time* 3rd November 1972

10. Conclusion

This book has been concerned with examining one particular method of work week restructuring, through the introduction of fwh. The inherent implication in this radical approach is that wage-earners in industrial society are going through a process of re-defining their role in society and that this finds expression in an increasing reluctance to accept the rigidity of a fixed working day.

But it would be wrong to imagine that work week changes will end with fwh. It has been claimed, for example, that a logical extension of fwh is the 4 day work week, but it is not our intention to consider that argument here. However, it is worth noting that, in some UK companies operating fwh, (with no limit on the number of half days off for credit time) the 4 day week has already become a reality. This is not without dangers and problems for management and workforce alike and the American experience (according to a recently published American Management Association report) indicates that organisations will do well to proceed slowly on this development.

Nevertheless, there is a discernible trend towards experimentation with work-week configurations and these are linked to the willingness of employees to accept a re-definition of the working day (if necessary as a *longer* day) in order to achieve objectives which include choice, flexibility and blocking of leisure time.

Initiation of these schemes is almost always by management and it appears that most employers have a double objective. On the one hand they wish to find a solution to dissatisfaction with work procedures in particular and alienation from industrial society in general; the argument being that this particular malaise expresses itself in low morale, high labour turnover, absenteeism and low efficiency. On the other hand, the objective may be higher productivity, cost reduction, better plant utilisation and improved company profitability. For most employers a combination of these motives, in a variety of mixes, would form desirable company objectives.

Despite the natural suspicion of employees to management-inspired change, it is significant that, in general, reaction to changes of this type, once initiated, have been highly favourable and

154

receptive. Whether the warmth of the reception is due to positive attitudes towards the need for the blocking of leisure time, or to the demand for more choice in work week structuring, is not quite clear. What is important is that employees, generally, appear to be ready to move more than half-way to meet their employers on these issues.

The attitudes of unions and other protective associations is less easily defined. Both on flexible working hours and four day working, unions have tended to adopt a highly conservative approach. Rarely do they take the initiative, preferring to *react* to movements by the employers. There is some evidence that ideological dogma may, in some cases, prevent them taking action which could have long term strategic advantages. Yet there is also evidence that, with the shift to company and plant bargaining, initiatives on the union side are more likely to come from the branch than from the centre. Nightshift workers in the car factories in Coventry decided, against the advice of their union leaders, that a four-night shift system was their choice — and the unions found no way of reversing their decision.

Finally, society in general will be interested in the results of the experiments now going on. But this will require more serious consideration than that given to the trends so far. What is required is an investigation carried out on the basis of systematic in-depth research, generating hard data which can be submitted to statistical analysis in terms of relevance and significance. This, we feel, must be the next stage and this book, hopefully, may have posed some of the questions to which such a study might find answers.

In the meantime the stream of firms and organisations installing flexible working hour systems may well become a flood. All the indications are that we are on the verge of one of the biggest structural alterations to the working week, since the battle for the 5 day week was won. The burden of persuasion, initiation and installation will fall upon a hardworking group of management executives both in personnel departments and management service units. It is for practitioners like these, that this book has been written.

Appendix I.
Four Sets of Rules

F.W.H. Rules - Example 1

Riker Laboratories — a factory application*

Riker Laboratories manufactures and markets a range of pharma-
ceutical and fine chemical products. Based in Loughborough,
Leicestershire the company has three establishments in the town,
consisting of two factories and its administrative headquarters.
Most of the company's products are manufactured at the Dishley
factory where approximately 160 persons are employed, including
45 laboratory staff. Flexible working was introduced at this
factory in November 1972 and, because of its early success, the
scheme was soon extended to include the administrative headquarters, employing over 200 staff, and the Wharncliffe Road
Factory where there is a high percentage of female labour,
working in teams on packaging lines. Over 550 employees enjoy
the facility of flexible working hours including all levels of staff.
At the time of writing (April 1973), the company was in the
process of reviewing the rules of its schemes, but those which
are reprinted here applied to the Dishley factory during the
initial three month trial. The company uses the Hengstler Flextime meter system for time recording.

Riker Laboratories
APPLICATION OF FLEXIBLE WORKING HOURS—FACTORY STAFF

1.   The Trial
The experimental scheme will operate from Monday 20 November for a
period of three months, towards the end of which Management will seek
the view of each employee.

   Depending on the success or failure of the trial, the Company reserves
the right to continue with the scheme or to revert to the present working
hours.

* Reproduced by kind permission of Riker Laboratories.

2. *The Working Day*

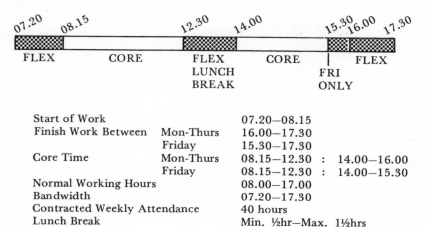

Start of Work		07.20—08.15
Finish Work Between	Mon-Thurs	16.00—17.30
	Friday	15.30—17.30
Core Time	Mon-Thurs	08.15—12.30 : 14.00—16.00
	Friday	08.15—12.30 : 14.00—15.30
Normal Working Hours		08.00—17.00
Bandwidth		07.20—17.30
Contracted Weekly Attendance		40 hours
Lunch Break		Min. ½hr—Max. 1½hrs

3. *Flexibility*

Each year will be split into four and five week periods (settlement periods). The contracted attendance during a settlement period is:

Number of weeks in settlement period x contracted weekly attendance, e.g. a four week settlement period = 160 hours

The permitted carryover, debit or credit, time to the next settlement period is five hours.

In addition to the use of Flextime for adjusting total hours worked, an employee can, with permission of his supervisor, take a full half day off in each settlement period, providing he does not exceed a five hour debit.

4. *Absence*

Permitted absence from work for medical and other than medical reasons will be unaffected by Flextime. However, employees making medical appointments should do their best to make them outside of Company time wherever possible. Holidays and other all day absences will count as a standard day, i.e. the contracted daily attendance. Part day absences will be calculated at standard rate for the day less time recorded on the meter.

5. *Limits to Flexibility*

Where employees form a team who depend on each other's presence for working efficiency, the members must agree on the working hours to be adopted by the team and advise their supervisor accordingly. If, within a bandwidth, a member of a team is ready to start work before the rest of the team, he may start to record time provided that:

(a) Permission of the supervisor is granted before time recording starts.
(b) There is a job that he can do.

Occasionally management may require employees to attend or leave at particular times to meet short-term demands of the job. Employees will be given advance notice wherever possible.

159

6. *Overtime*

Present arrangements for overtime will be unaffected by Flextime. Overtime is at the specific request of the Departmental Manager. Overtime hours will be recorded on the time clock as previously.

7. *Tea Breaks*

Employees may continue to take tea breaks as at present. Whilst it remains that all staff will be expected to take a morning tea break of a minimum of fifteen minutes, the afternoon break will be optional, enabling staff to build up Flextime credits if this is their desire. Within reason, the morning and afternoon breaks may be extended and the latter may be shortened.

To enable this flexibility of breaks it will be necessary for employees to use the time recorders when they take a break by withdrawing their personal keys.

8. *Preparation for Work — Washing Allowance*

At the present time employees are allowed three minutes at the beginning and three minutes at the end of both morning and afternoon for preparing for, and washing hands after work. With Flextime employees will be credited with an equivalent allowance of twelve minutes per day, i.e. one hour per week for this.

9. *Time Recording*

Each employee is allocated a time counter and will be issued with a personal coded key which activates the time counter, sited wherever possible in individual departments. If this scheme is continued after the trial the key will become the Security Pass.

When an employee leaves the factory premises, his key must be removed from his time recorder and re-inserted on his return. The time spent away from the factory must be recorded on the department's 'Absence from Site' sheet and initialled by the supervisor.

If an employee forgets his key, he may obtain a duplicate from his departmental manager for use during that day, which must be returned to the supervisor when the employee finishes work. A red master key enabling any time recorder to be switched on will be kept by the Factory Manager and may be used when, for special reasons, neither the employee's personal key nor the duplicate key is available.

If at the end of a day an employee leaves his key in the meter by mistake it will be removed by a security guard and will be returned to the receptionist for collection by the individual's supervisor the following morning. Any necessary adjustment to the hours recorded will be entered on the 'Absence from Site' sheet and initialled by the supervisor.

10. *Documentation of attendance and absences*

(a) Absences

Every week an 'Absence from Site' sheet will be initiated in each department to record the occasions when employees are absent from work or away from the Dishley site.

The information required on the sheet is:

Date	Name	Reason For Absence	From	To	Total Time		Approved By	Pay Instructions
					hrs	1/100Hr		

*The pay instructions will be completed and the sheet approved by the departmental manager at the end of each week before forwarding it to the receptionist.

Examples of absence from site for which an entry is required:

    Holidays
    Sick Leave
    Inter site visits
    Medical and other appointments made in core time
    Away on company business
    Training activities at the Training Centre
    Attendance at a day release course of Further Education

Pads of pre-printed 'Absence from Site' sheets will be issued to departmental managers.

For those employees who by nature of their jobs are required to leave the site on many occasions, alternative arrangements for time recording are planned which will be explained to them individually.

(b) Meter Reading Recording:

Every Friday, before employees finish work, they are required to record their meter readings on a 'Flextime Record Sheet', sited next to the meter. Their entries will be checked by the security guard who will remove the sheet and pass it to the receptionist for calculation. The employee will be informed by means of a paper slip of his or her debit or credit hours, on the Monday or Tuesday of the succeeding week.

The slip will show the following information:

Name	Meter Reading		Credit or Debit				Week No	No.of Weeks in Period
			This Week		This Month			
	Hrs	1/100Hr	Hrs	1/100Hr	Hrs	1/100Hr		

Any queries regarding the calculation should be directed to the appropriate supervisor.

If an employee is absent on a Friday his meter reading will be recorded by the appropriate supervisor.

Meters will be re-set to zero at the end of each week.

11. *Miscellaneous*

All staff will appreciate that the overriding consideration must be the completion of work. Therefore, it will not always be possible to take advantage of Flextime on a particular day.

The whole concept of introducing Flextime is intended to improve working conditions for employees. However, with Flextime an individual employee may decide to carry on working the same hours as at present without loss of any existing benefits.

Abuse of the equipment introduced in connection will be regarded as grounds for instant termination of employment.

F.W.H. Rules - Example 2

**The Cascelloid Division of Bakelite Xylonite Ltd —
An Office Application***

The Cascelliod Division of Bakelite Xylonite Ltd, Leicester introduced Flexible Working for their office staff in August 1972. There are approximately one hundred employees taking part in this scheme, although it has now been extended into other areas of the company.

The system of time recording is by means of a time clock which was supplied by International Time Recording Ltd and prior to the introduction of the scheme the staff were not required to 'clock in'.

(Note: 1 unit = 6 minutes)

1.   *Core Time*
Except in special circumstances or as outlined in (2) everyone must be present during the periods 09.30—12.30; 14.30—16.00 each day.

2.   *Absence Involving Core Time*
This may arise for personal or Company reasons.

Absence will not count as debit time when the employee is ill (as covered by Staff Conditions) or on holiday, or given special permission to be absent. i.e. jury service, death of member of immediate family (immediate family means Husband/Wife, Father/Mother, Children).

Treatment at hospital, if required more than twice per week *and* for more than three consecutive weeks, will also incur no debit.

Absence on Company business will normally incur no debits or credits, but journeys of more than 200 miles in one day, will attract an additional credit of 30 units (3 hours).

In addition there will be a credit of 20 units (2 hours), when absence overnight on Company business is authorised: this is not available on any day in which the credit in the previous paragraph applies.

Leave granted for any other reason, will count as a debit of the actual time lost — this includes visits to the dentist, doctor or hospital (other than for treatment as outlined earlier), and all forms of personal business.

* Reproduced by kind permission of Cascelloid Division of B.L.X. Ltd.

3. *Flexible Time*
Subject to (11), employees may take advantage of the undermentioned periods for commencing and leaving the site.

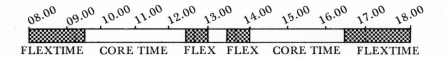

4. *Contracted Hours*
Each employee must fulfill his contracted hours in any settlement period, subject only to (6).
Contracted hours = 7½ hours (75 units) x number of working days in any calendar month.

5. *Settlement Period*
A Calendar month.

6. *Debit/Credit hours — complete month*
Carry forward allowed up to maximum 10 hours, from one settlement period to another.

Credit balances are not overtime (see 7) but hours worked to provide more flexibility in the following settlement period.

A person leaving the Company would be expected to create a 'ZERO' debit /credit prior to the last week of the expiry of notice, and to work 8.45 am-1.00 pm, 2.00 pm — 5.15 pm during the last week.

7. *Overtime*
Additional time worked at the request of the employee's Manager, will only be paid as overtime if it satisfies the undermentioned conditions.
(a)   Total working hours in any day must be at least 8½ before any over-time payment may be authorised for that day, but the fact that 8½ hours have been worked, does not of itself, imply payment for additional hours.
Overtime cannot be authorised retrospectively.
(b)   Any short fall in contracted hours worked in any settlement period in which overtime is operated, will be deducted from the authorised over-time hours and overtime payment will only be made for the remainder (if any).
Hours worked in a settlement period over and above the maximum carry forward of 10 hours are disallowed and do not count as overtime unless they comply with the conditions in the previous paragraphs.
Overtime hours must be recorded on the weekly authorisation form by the Departmental Manager.

8. *Attendance Recording*
There is a need for objective attendance recording — *not to control punctuality*

164

but to enable management and the employee to see where he stands. It is very important to realise that, other than in core time, *no one can be late* and the record is quite simply to credit and debit hours of attendance accurately.

Special automatic time clocks are provided.

ALL departures and/or returns to the site, *MUST* be recorded.

9. *Attendance Recording — Special Calculations*

(a) If travelling on Company business without first commencing work at the office, an artificial commencing time of 12 units will be used, together with actual units recorded for lunch and/or evening.

   If leaving the site during the day on Company business but not returning on the same day, an artificial finishing time of 97 units will be used, together with actual clocking for lunch and/or morning.

(b) Half Day Holiday

   For a zero rating, 37 units must be achieved in the worked part of the day. Units less or more than 37 count as a debit or credit to Flextime.

10. *Use of Credits*

Credits may either be used to adjust your working day as allowed under (3) or up to two half days or one full day may be taken against time credits brought forward from the previous month, providing previous Managerial approval has been obtained.

11. *Responsibility to the Job*

The success of Flextime depends upon a responsible attitude of each employee to his job i.e. the job comes first.

F.W.H. Rules - Example 3

Legal and General Assurance Society Ltd

One of the three Head Offices of the Legal and General Assurance Society Ltd is sited at Kingswood, Surrey and it stands amid farm-land and playing fields. Flexible working was introduced in October 1972 and because of its success it was adopted perman-ently on 1 April 1973.

There are 1,600 employees participating in the scheme and this is probably the longest trial carried out in the UK so far. The meter recording system that is used was supplied by Hengstler Flextime Ltd.

Flextime Rules

1. Working hours may commence at any time between 8.15 am and 10.00 am and cease at any time between 4.00 pm and 6.15 pm.

2. Attendance between 10.00 am and 4.00 pm is mandatory.

3. On commencement of work a staff member should insert his key card in his allocated space in the recorder. The key card should be withdrawn immediately on ceasing work, during any interruption of work in ab-sence from the office for personal reasons and during the lunch interval.

4. The lunch interval should be of at least 30 minutes duration. It should not exceed one hour unless prior departmental permission has been obtained.
   Staff must leave working areas of the office during this interval.

5. The key card should be removed from the recorder before commencing paid overtime work. Overtime hours for payment will be reduced by the amount of any shortfall in contracted hours worked during a month subject to the provisions of Rule 10.

*Reproduced by kind permission of Legal and General Assurance Society Ltd

Paid overtime may be authorised by an Official at not less than Controller level. The total working hours must be at least 9 (excluding the lunch interval but including 15 minutes tea break) on any day in which payment is to be made for overtime.

6. Absence on business should be separately recorded as for overtime unless within the normal working day when key cards can be inserted and removed from the recorder.

7. Medical treatment and advice must often of necessity be within normal working hours. Time credits may then be approved in suitable cases but not in respect of absence for usual periodic dental treatment.

8. Holidays and sick leave which are to rank as working hours should be manually recorded.

9. Every staff member must work the full number of contracted hours during each calendar month less approved credits as in Paragraphs 6, 7 and 8 and subject to the provisions of Paragraph 10. Contracted hours for most staff are 7 in respect of each working day during the calendar month.

10. The accumulated hours worked by each individual will be read from the recorder and noted by departments on the last working day of each calendar month and the recorders will then be reset to zero.

11. Debits and credits of up to 7 hours only in the number of contracted hours worked may be carried forward from one month to the next.

12. A maximum of one day's or two half days' holiday may be taken during a calendar month subject to departmental permission. Such holiday should normally be met from excess hours already worked to date and must never place the staff member concerned more than 7 hours in current debit.

13. Time credits will not normally be granted in the event of lateness in arrival at the office due to traffic delays or other travel hazards. In such circumstances, however, there may be suspension of mandatory working hours and debits of more than 7 hours may be carried forward from one month to the next but only subject to the approval of Personnel Department.

14. The operation of Flextime must always be subject to work requirements but the staff will be given as much warning as possible by Departmental Officials when any limitations must temporarily be imposed on the flexibility of hours.

15. Any relaxation in these Rules may be made only with the approval of Personnel Department.

16. Office Services Department are responsible for the master clock units at Head Office including their alteration to and from summer and winter time.

17. The Association Room at St. Monica's will be open at times as arranged with the Committee of the Social and Athletic Association. Other Association facilities within St. Monica's, except for changing accommodation, will not be available to members until 5.15 pm.
    Recreational facilities within the grounds may be used only after 4.00 pm on ceasing work.

18. Staff members undertaking duties on behalf of the Social and Athletic Association must do so in their own leisure times unless an arrangement has first been approved by the Departmental Head for the loan of services with appropriate charge to the Association.

19. The Flextime system is of particular value to those staff members who undertake voluntary service and social commitments of various descriptions. An allowance of office time cannot be made in respect of this service other than under the Rules laid down for members of the Armed Forces.

20. Absence from the office for purposes of training off the job should be limited to a maximum of 7 hours in respect of each working day involved.

21. Credit may be granted in respect of hours worked after 6.15 pm, when this is undertaken with permission at not less than Controller level and when the time involved does not form part of approved paid overtime.

22. Staff members may be required to produce key cards as proof of identity in the Staff Restaurant or elsewhere on office premises.

23. Staff members under notice of termination or resignation must not allow their contracted hours worked to fall into debit during the notice period. Should this occur, delay may arise in payment of the final salary entitlement with deduction as appropriate to final debit hours.

24. A monthly return will be made to Personnel Department of the names of staff failing to observe mandatory hours or who show a deficiency in the number of hours worked beyond the permitted variation of 7 hours.

25. On arrival and departure do not disturb colleagues already or still at work.

26. At the sole discretion of Management, Flextime may be discontinued as a whole or in individual cases at any time.

    N.B. No rule has been included to cover the request of the Actuary that credits of more than 7 hours should be carried forward from month to month. The point might be covered under Rule 15 but if firm approval is to be given to such an arrangement it is probably better specifically covered.

F.W.H. Rules - Example 4

Essex River Authority*

The Essex River Authority introduced Flexible Working on 5 June 1972 for staff working in the Treasurer's Department and Head Office in Chelmsford and the River Conservators and Treasurer's staff at their Northern office in Colchester. The scheme has now been extended to approximately 300 employees including supervisory staff of civil engineering work. A meter system of time recording is used.

Rules

ESSEX RIVER AUTHORITY
Flextime Scheme Working Conditions
1. The following conditions will apply to staff who are working Flextime. Staff Joint consultation will be maintained at all times and copies of amendments agreed distributed down to section level.

2. Flextime divides the working day into two parts:—
   (a) a fixed period during which all officers must be at work ('core time')
   (b) a flexible period during which the officer has some discretion in attending at work ('flextime')
   The freedom to decide when to start and finish work each day will be subject to the provision that each officer works the requisite number of hours per week, and that peak or other work demands are satisfied as and when they occur.

3. For the purposes of the scheme the working day has been divided as follows:—

Flexible hours	8.00— 9.15
Core time	9.15—12.00
Flexible hours	12.00—12.45
Fixed lunch break	12.45— 1.15
Flexible hours	1.15— 2.00
Core time	2.00— 4.15
Flexible hours	4.15— 6.00

   A four week accounting period will be used to give a total number of

* Reproduced by kind permission of the Essex River Authority

hours per period as 38 x 4 = 152 (less any statutory holidays occurring within the period). When the shorter working week is introduced the total number of hours per period will be 37 x 4 = 148 (or for the Romford Office only, 36 x 4 = 144).

4. The Authority's nominal business hours for sections which have to be manned for internal or external responsibilities will be as follows:—
   From 8.1.73
   8.30 — 12.30   1.45 — 5.15
   From Implementation of 37/36 Hour Week
   8.30 — 12.30   1.45 — 5.00 (4.45 Fridays)
   These hours must not be confused with normal working hours for officers not on Flextime.

5. The following guidelines have been agreed for the effective working of the scheme:—
   (a)   The *general* pattern of working hours for the individual officer (normally applicable for a four week period) shall be such as may be agreed with the section head. The section head has discretion to authorise departure from that pattern of time to time.
   (b)   In any four week period a *maximum* of minus 4 or plus 8 hours deviation from the requisite number of hours within the accounting period will be allowed. The actual deviation (or the maximum limit of plus 8 hours if this is exceeded in the case of credits) will be added to or subtracted from the hours required to be worked in the next accounting period. The permitted debit balance may not be exceeded and staff are advised that difficulties could arise in some instances, due to manning requirements etc., in the transfer of the higher credit balances.
   (c)   Emergency absences may be authorised by the section head in core time. Routine dental appointments should be fixed to Flextime.
   (d)   Overtime is limited to *authorised* work outside the 8.00 am — 6.00 pm working day, leaving unaffected the above mentioned working obligations within those hours. Any officer with authorised overtime *as defined above* will have the option of receiving overtime payment (if this is applicable to the officer's grade), or of having time off in lieu credited during flex or core time (provided that prior permission for time off has been obtained from the section head.

6. *Recording of Hours*
   To reduce the amount of calculations and paper work involved in Flextime working, it has been agreed that electro-mechanical recording equipment will be used. A control unit activates a number of individual time counters within the stipulated flextime and core time periods. Each officer will be given a keyed plastic card which is inserted into the slot of a given time counter on the recording unit, as soon as the officer arrives at the office, The insertion of the plastic card will activate the individual's time counter to record cumulatively the hours spent at the office (excluding the fixed lunch period). When the officer leaves the premises the plastic card is removed from the slot and the counter stops recording. The equipment is

not a "clocking in" system inasmuch as *starting and leaving times are not recorded* and the officer can at any time see the cumulative number of hours worked during the four-week accounting period. The time is recorded in decimal hours.

In order to deal with time spent away from the office, additional manual recording will be required and the officer will record periods of outside duty, authorised absence, sickness, training etc. so that the total cumulative hours for the period can be calculated. When the authorised absence extends to a complete day or a half day the following hours will be credit on the record sheet:

Standard Working Week	Full Day	Morning or Afternoon
38 hours	7.6 hours	3.8 hours
37 "	7.4 "	3.7 "
36 "	7.2 "	3.6 "

7. Supplementary notes on the scheme may be issued by individual sections to cover local conditions or special requirements.

8. The scheme will commence at 8.00 am on Monday the 8th January 1973.

Appendix II.
A Company-Union Agreement
(See Chapter 9)

A Flexihour System

An Agreement between London and Manchester Assurance Company Limited and Association of Scientific, Technical and Managerial Staffs.

1. *Introduction*
    1.1 The London and Manchester will introduce a flexihour system in October 1972. The scheme is designed to give employees as much freedom to decide their hours of work as is possible while giving a good service to our clients and meeting the needs of our field staff.
    1.2 After the scheme has been in operation for four months the Joint Consultative Commitee will discuss its advantages and disadvantages and consider any amendments which may be necessary in the light of our experience.
    1.3 All employees will come under the administrative arrangements whether they wish to take advantage of the flexihour system or not. This will include management as well as staff.
    1.4 The increased freedom that this system gives also brings greater responsibility to all concerned. The manner in which individuals exercise that freedom will determine the success of the scheme.
    1.5 It is appreciated that some sections and/or departments will be able to take greater advantage of the new system than others. Members must accept the responsibilities of the departments to which they belong.
    1.6 This Agreement is solemnly binding in honour but it is not intended to give rise to any legal obligations.

2. *The Role of the Departmental Manager*
    Managers must exercise particular care that the work of their departments does not suffer as a result of introducing this scheme. It may indeed be possible to improve the efficiency of a department by consultation with the staff. The manager must consider the following requirements:
    2.1 Work is available for those working outside the normal hours.
    2.2 The communication system is satisfactory
    2.3 Deadlines of work for all sections are met.

2.4 Other sections/departments are not affected adversely.
2.5 Cover is adequate during normal office hours.
2.6 Satisfactory supervision is available where necessary.
2.7 No member of staff is left alone in potentially dangerous circumstances.
Note: Attention is drawn to the grievance procedure for any member of the staff who feels they are being unreasonably prevented from taking advantage of the scheme.

3. *Description of the scheme*
   3.1 The hours permitted in the scheme will be as follows:
     (a) Staff may start work between the hours of 8.00 and 10.00.
     (b) Morning core time is 10.00 to 12.00
     (c) The lunch time break is 12.00 to 15.00 with a minimum of half an hour. No lunches will be served after 14.30.
     (d) Afternoon core time is from 15.00 to 16.00
     (e) Staff may leave between 16.00 and 19.00.
   3.2 The maximum working day will be limited to 9 hours.
   3.3 Staff cannot be compelled to work outside the present normal working hours if they do not wish to do so.
   3.4 Any work done in time outside the flexihours must be specifically authorised by Personnel unless under established arrangements (e.g. computer shift-work).
   3.5 Overtime will be dealt with entirely separately from the scheme. Staff will record the time of finishing the normal working period.
Note: All arrangements are subject to paragraph 2 above.

4. Machines will be sited close to the central lifts on each floor for automatically recording times.
   4.1 Employees will record the time of commencement and finish of each session. Morning and afternoon will be considered as separate sessions. Entries will also show a personal number for identification.
   4.2 Staff working outside the office will submit returns to their manager showing the actual work period under— taken. Travelling time will not normally be included unless it is essential to return to Chief Office.
   4.3 Credit time outstanding will be reported weekly. It will then be taken by arrangement with the manager.

4.4 At the end of each four week period the time under or over standard work time will be reported. No more than 10 hours either way may be carried over into the next month except by prior agreement with or at the specific request of the manager.

4.5 If employees forget to sign on or off the onus of proving their times of attendance will be on them.

5. *Crediting of Hours*
This will happen in the following circumstances:

5.1 7 hours per day for holidays (3½ hours per half day).

5.2 7 hours per day for sickness. If taken ill during the day the balance of 7 hours not worked will be allowed.

5.3 The number of hours appropriated to the individual circumstances of the case as agreed with the manager for hospital visits and dental treatment.

5.4 Day release according to agreed times.

5.5 Organised interference with public transport will be dealt with sympathetically in the knowledge that staff will respond by working to mitigate the effects as in the past by taking short lunch times, taking work home and putting in special effort.

6. *Definitions*

6.1 Normal office hours are defined as 09.00 to 17.00 with 1 hour for lunch.

6.2 Core time is that period during which all the staff attending the office for the session are present at the same time. Subject to all the provisos in paragraph 2 the scheme does not compel staff to attend any particular session or sessions in the week.

6.3 Debit time outstanding equals the standard hours for the working days in the four week period less time worked and less any time credited under Section 5.

6.4 Credit time equals the time worked in the four week period, plus time credited under section 5, less the total standard hours for that working period.

7. *Termination of Employment*
On the termination of employment allowance will be made at the normal salary rate for any hours credited subject to a maximum of ten hours. If there is time debited to the

employee this will be treated as time off without pay (ie a deduction will be made based on hours debited multiplied by the normal hourly salary rate).

Signed on behalf of
the Company

Signed on behalf of
the Union

22/9/72

Appendix III.
U.K. Manufacturers of Flexible Time RecordingEquipment
(See Chapter 4)

1. *Conventional Time Clocks (suitably adapted for fwh)*
    Blick Time Recorders Ltd
    Blick House
    44/46 Sekforde Street
    London EC1   Tel: 01-253 5224

    International Time Recording Co. Ltd.
    PO Box 726
    Beavor Lane
    Hammersmith
    London W6 9AR   Tel: 01-748 4484

    Simplex Time Recorder Company
    62 Wilbury Way
    Hitchen
    Herts   Tel: 0462 52081

    Telephone Rentals Ltd
    197 Knightsbridge
    London SW7 1RL   Tel 01-589 1471

2. *Meter Systems*
    Hasler (G.B.) Ltd.
    Commerce Way
    Croydon CR0 4XA   Tel: 01-686 0901

    Hengstler Flextime Ltd
    Abbey Chambers
    Highbridge Street
    Waltham Abbey
    Essex   Tel: 0992 26166

    Northgate Instruments Ltd
    Selectatime Division
    19 London Road
    Gloucester GL1 3EZ   Tel: 0452 21369

3. *Computerised Badge Reader Systems*
    Addo Ltd
    85 Great North Road
    Hatfield
    Herts   Tel: 070 72 63511

    British Olivetti Ltd.
    30 Berkeley Square
    London W1X 6AH   Tel: 01-629 8807

    Feedback Data Ltd
    Bell Brook
    Uckfield
    Sussex   Tel: 0825 4222

    Telephone Rentals Ltd
    197 Knightsbirdge
    London SW7 1RL   Tel: 01-589 1471

Index